Turn Your Magic into a Beautiful Expression of Power

Used for millennia in countries all over the world, henna is one of the most powerful plants for herbalism and mystical ritual. *Henna Magic* will introduce you to the mysteries and magical uses of this sacred form of body art and offer you a wonderful new way to enhance your spirituality and spellcraft.

Begin your journey with a fascinating history of the henna plant and its traditional and contemporary uses in various cultures. Then discover how to create original henna tattoos that resonate with your spiritual intention. In clear, easy-to-follow steps, you will learn to mix henna paste, blend in herbs and oils that correspond to your magical purpose, prepare the skin for application, and create unique designs for any occasion, ritual, or spell.

You'll also find design ideas for specific areas of the body, a list of symbols with concise explanations of their significance and meanings, and a thorough exploration of magical, planetary, herbal, and elemental correspondences.

Henna Magic

Chris Lee

About the Author

Philippa Faulks (Norwich, United Kingdom) studies herbology, ancient religions, and anthropology, with a special focus on ancient Egypt and the Middle East. She is the author of four books whose subjects include Freemasonry, magic, and meditation.

Visit her online at www.philippafaulks.co.uk.

Henna Magic

Crafting Charms & Rituals
with Sacred Body Art

Philippa Faulks

Llewellyn Publications
Woodbury, Minnesota

FIRST EDITION
First Printing, 2010

Book design by Rebecca Zins

Cover design and henna image used on pages i, v, and 268 by Lisa Novak

Illustrations by Llewellyn Art Department except for sidebar ornament
and illustrations on pages vii, 51, 61, 63–69, 170, and 195 by Philippa Faulks

Henna plant on page 23 from *Medieval Herb, Plant and Flower Illustrations*
by Carol Belanger Grafton (Dover Publications ©2004); owl image on page 96
from *Magic and Mystical Symbols* (Dover Publications ©2004)

Library of Congress Cataloging-in-Publication Data
Faulks, Philippa.
  Henna magic : crafting charms & rituals with sacred body art /
Philippa Faulks.—1st ed.
       p. cm.
  Includes bibliographical references and index.
  ISBN 978-0-7387-1915-3
  1. Body marking—Religious aspects. 2. Henna (Dye) 3. Magic. 4.
Rites and ceremonies. I. Title.
  GN419.15.F38 2010
  391.6´5—dc22
                                2010035233

Llewellyn Worldwide Ltd. does not participate in, endorse, or have any authority or responsibility concerning private business transactions between our authors and the public.

All mail addressed to the author is forwarded, but the publisher cannot, unless specifically instructed by the author, give out an address or phone number.

Any Internet references contained in this work are current at publication time, but the publisher cannot guarantee that a specific location will continue to be maintained. Please refer to the publisher's website for links to authors' websites and other sources.

Llewellyn Publications
A Division of Llewellyn Worldwide Ltd.
2143 Wooddale Drive
Woodbury, MN 55125-2989
www.llewellyn.com

Printed in the United States of America

This book is dedicated to
the henna djinn
&
my beautiful daughter,
of whom I am so proud

Contents

Acknowledgments   xvii

Important Information: Black Henna/PPD Warning   xix

Introduction   1

CHAPTER 1   *Henna   5*

What Is Henna?   5

A Plant of Many Names   7

So Where Did It Come From?   8

What Was Henna Used For?   9

Healing Henna   10

Henna, Hair, and Nails   12

Henna's Sacred Art   14

All-Purpose Henna   17

CHAPTER 2   *Magic   19*

So What Is Magic?   19

The Magical Basics   20

    Ground Rule #1: Harm No Other   21

    Ground Rule #2: Avoid Outward Manipulation of Another's Will   21

    Ground Rule #3: Keep Your Magic to Yourself   21

Can Anyone Do It?   21

A Magical Web: Weaving the Wisdom   22

It's a Kind of Magic!   23

Sympathetic Magic   24

Making Magic: The Mystical Melting Pot   24

    Symbols   24

    Scents and Senses   25

    Amulets, Charms, and Talismans   25

What Is Ritual, and Why Do We Do It?   26

Correspondences: What Are They, Which Do I Use,
    and When Do I Use Them?   27

CHAPTER 3   *Henna Magic Through the Ages   31*

Henna's Journey   31

Henna in India   32

Henna in Africa, the Middle East, and Islam   33

Henna in Jewish Cultures   37

Henna Rituals in History and Beyond   37

    Pregnancy and Childbirth   37

    Circumcision   39

    Weddings   41

    Death and Funerals   47

    War   48

Festivals   49

    Karwa Chauth   49

    Ramadan and Eid al-Fitr   49

    Eid al-Adha   50

    Purim   50

    Henna for Animals   51

Henna and the Djinn   52
    Protection and Attraction   52
Purification   55
    A Trip to the Hammam   55
    Ritual Ablutions   57

CHAPTER 4   *Charms, Talismans & Symbols   59*
Blessed Henna   59
Protection: The Curse of the Evil Eye   60
Where to Place Your Henna Design   62
    Hands and Fingers   63
    Wrist and Lower Arm   66
    Upper Arm and Shoulder   66
    Back and Shoulders   66
    Legs and Ankles   67
    Soles of the Feet   67
    Top of the Foot   68
    Neck and Décolletage   69
    Breasts   69
    Solar Plexus   69
    Belly   70
Common Symbols: Their Meanings and Uses   71

CHAPTER 5   *Herbs and Oils in Henna Magic   111*
Almost Alchemy, 111
    Obtaining Your Herbs and Oils, 112
    Using Herbs and Oils with Power, 112

A Guide to the Uses of Magical Herbs and Oils, 113

    Astrological   *114*

    Gods & Goddesses   *115*

    Happiness   *116*

    Healing   *117*

    Love   *120*

    Planets   *122*

    Protection   *123*

    Purification   *126*

    Spiritual Work   *128*

    Wealth & Prosperity   *129*

CHAPTER 6   *Magical Correspondences*   *133*

    Let's Start at the Very Beginning...   133

    Constructing a Ritual   *134*

    Moon Phases   *135*

    The Correspondences   135

    Elemental   *136*

    Planetary   *140*

    Astrological   *145*

    Angelic   *152*

CHAPTER 7   *A Henna Ritual: the Application*   *157*

    Types of Henna   157

    How Does Henna Stain, and How Long Will It Last?   163

    Getting Started   166

Equipment   169
    Cones, Bottles, and Brushes   169
Henna Recipes: A Step-by-Step Guide to Mixing Your Paste   172
    Really Simple Henna Paste   173
    How to Fill Your Cone or Bottle   175
    Terpene-Rich Henna Paste   176
    Farah's Recipe   179
    Lemon and Sugar Glaze   180
Applying Your Design: A Step-by-Step Guide   181
    Preparing the Skin for Decoration   181
    Have Everything You Need at Hand   181
    Equipment   183
    How to Use a Bottle or Cone   184
    Using an Eye Pencil   187
    Using Stencils   187
    Using Transfer Paper   188
Applying the Henna   188
    Preserving Your Work   188
    Removing Henna Stains   192

CHAPTER 8   *Henna Spells   193*
Creating Your Designs   194
The Spells   196
    Oils   197
    Flowers, Herbs & Powders   197
    To Prepare   197

Beauty   199

Happiness   200

Health & Healing   201

Love   203

Protection   206

Purification   208

Sacred Spirituality   209

Wealth & Prosperity   210

CHAPTER 9   *Henna Rituals*   *213*

Engagement, Wedding, or Handfasting   213

Ancient Egypt   214

Indian Dreams   215

Turkish Delight   215

Pregnancy or Baby Shower   217

Purification Ritual   219

Erotic Ritual   221

Celebration Henna Ritual: For Good Luck, Leaving Home,
Coming Home, Birthdays, or Anniversaries   223

Making a Magical Mehndi Cake   223

How to Mehndi Your Cake   226

Other Fun Things to Do for Henna Parties   227

Passing Ritual: For the Deceased, the Living, and the Grieving   228

Anointing the Dying: The Henna Ritual of Peace   229

Anointing the Dead: The Henna Ritual of Transition   231

Magical Henna Journal   233

Bibliography   235

Appendix: Henna Resources & Information   239

Recommended Reading   251

Index   255

Acknowledgments

A project like this can never be done alone, and I am lucky enough to have been inspired, helped, and given encouragement by many who have become new friends. My gratitude and appreciation goes to everyone who helped in any way.

Firstly, my thanks go to the team at Llewellyn Worldwide, especially Elysia Gallo and Rebecca Zins, for their insight and belief in the magic of henna.

But my deepest gratitude goes to those who have offered their help gratis and with great encouragement: Alex Morgan of Spellstone for her sublime artwork and designs; the "henna girls"—henna artists Farah Khan, Sarah Ali Khan, Amrit Bansal, Maggie Johnston, and Darcy V—for letting me use photographs throughout the book of their beautiful henna work; and photographer Ro Lee-Foyster for her patience and skill in capturing the alchemy at work. Special thanks must go to Catherine Cartwright-Jones for creating the Henna Pages and all its accompanying work, for without her tireless research and passionate love of henna, we would all be lost for inspiration and knowledge on the subject. Thanks also to Joe James and Claire Watts for testing the henna pens so creatively.

Last but not least, my eternal love and thanks to my husband and daughter for their continual support and encouragement, even when I was a "henna hermit" during the writing of the book.

Important Information
Black Henna/PPD Warning

In recent times, there has been increasing use of a substance called "black henna" to attempt to achieve very dark, temporary "henna" tattoos—this is NOT henna. It is often a mixture of black hair dye incorporating PPD (paraphenylenediamine), which can be, at the least, irritating to the skin—but in more serious cases, it can cause allergic reactions (including respiratory or organ failure) and/or severe skin burns. PPD or other additives may even be added to red henna, so it is very important to use pure henna.

Please do not use this substance; only purchase henna that comes from a reputable retailer. I have included details of some of the best suppliers in the appendix at the back of the book.

It is also wise to avoid using henna on children under five, as its use for large applications (e.g., palm, head, etc.) has been linked to blood cell depletion leading to hyperbilirubinemia. In the case of children with G6PD (glucose-6-phosphate dehydrogenase) deficiency, henna can cause serious risk of illness or death and should be avoided.

For pregnancy, henna is generally safe to use after the first trimester, but not all essential oils are safe; please refer to chapter 3 for further information or consult your obstetrician.

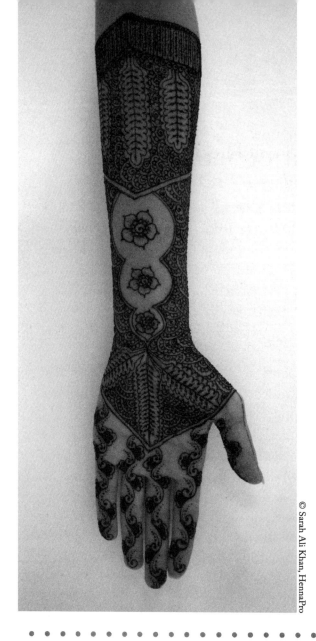

Full arm henna

Introduction

The use of henna conjures up different images for different people. For some, the flaming red of hennaed hair is the most enduring image, often associated with the hippy era; others remember the delicate tracings on hands and feet that are used for festivals and weddings in the Middle Eastern and Indian cultures. In fact, henna has been used globally for decoration, medicine, and cosmetic use for over 5,000 years, and it is an enduring practice that has not lost its powerful beauty and mystery. In this book, I hope to give you a glimpse of the history, usage, and symbolism of this perennially magical plant.

For Westerners, the ceremony that we tend to associate henna decoration with is, of course, the wedding. We all have seen the pictures of beautiful Indian brides delicately covered in the intricate and symbolic tracery of *mehndi*—the Indian name for henna body decoration—to convey blessings of good luck and love for the couple.

Body art is a timeless tradition, and in one way or another, people from all over the world have found ways to adorn themselves either to enhance their natural beauty or to create a symbolic meaning. Tribal scarring, tattoos, piercings, and body painting have occurred universally for thousands of years and modernly are becoming popular in Western cultures. Nothing is really new in the invention of body art, but there are those of us who would like to be able to decorate ourselves without pain, mutilation, or branding ourselves with a design for the rest of our lives. This is where henna is the perfect tool: it is semipermanent, nontoxic,

Bridal henna, above;
delicate hand henna, right;
hennaed foot, opposite page

and painless. The paste, when applied and left on the skin, permeates the epidermal layers and leaves a stain that can last anywhere from seven days to six weeks, depending on aftercare, and so is perfect for those wishing to decorate themselves for a special occasion or for a ritual practice—as the stain fades, the work is done!

I first used henna as a hair dye over twenty-five years ago and was fascinated by its amazing staining power (I think my mother was too, as she was the one who used to wash the towels)! When I started researching for this book, I was mainly interested in the use of henna as decoration. Delving further, though, I have since been drawn intrinsically into its web of beautifully steeped history. It has now become an enigma to me, and I am forever searching for more information on this incredibly indelible plant. I hope that in the following pages, you too will fall in love with the amazing power of henna.

Included in this book are designs, spells, and fun ideas to give you inspiration to create modern magical adornment for you and others. The potent mixture of a sacred plant with a millennium of use and ancient symbols and serious intent can

impart a powerful magical reaction. It doesn't matter what faith, religion, or creed you aspire to; the magic of henna is perennial and universal, suitable for all. As you will discover, henna as a mystical tool has penetrated the religions of Judaism, Christianity, Islam, and many, many other traditions and faiths. It has no bias, no prejudice, and is a catalyst for change. So this wisdom is not only for the serious magician but for anyone who wishes to turn a celebration or a ritual into a beautiful expression of power—in other words, for you to become a living talisman. Happy hennaing!

Henna

Your plants are an orchard of pomegranates
With pleasant fruits,
Fragrant henna with spikenard,
Spikenard and saffron,
Calamus and cinnamon,
With all trees of frankincense,
Myrrh and aloes,
With all the chief spices . . .
—The Song of Solomon 4:13–14

- -

What Is Henna?

Henna is a plant that has been used for thousands of years as a medicinal aid and to make a dye for staining skin, hair, nails, cloth, and animal skins.

Botanically known as *Lawsonia inermis,* it has dark green leaves, bears delicate white flowers, and has a growing height of up to ten feet. Other variants can produce pink, red, or yellow blossoms. These blossoms are beautifully fragrant and have long been used as perfume. The Prophet Muhammad claimed it was his favorite scent. Henna blossom attar, or essential oil, is known as Gulhina and is usually produced in India.

While henna is an arid-climate-loving plant, it can now be found in the tropical or subtropical regions of Africa, southern Asia, and Australasia. The parts of the plant used for dye or medicine are from the dried petioles, or leavestock, and leaves. Mostly produced in India and Africa, this dried powder can now be found for sale around the world. There is some plant variation from region to region due to the differing climates and soil conditions, and it is said that henna has different colouring properties dependent on its origin of growth. The dried powder is naturally of various greenish-brown hues, and the resulting stain ranges from orange to brick red to deep brown. Even though "black henna" is often offered to tourists, there is no such thing as a natural black henna, and the resulting black stain is caused by mixing henna with chemicals, often simply the potent chemical PPD on its own, which presents serious health hazards.

The actual powder is manufactured by drying and crushing the leaves from the henna bush, which is then sifted to remove debris. Good-quality henna powder is best when it comes from one country of origin, though quite often powder from several countries is blended to keep the price lower.

A Plant of Many Names

Henna is one of the most universally used and loved plants; virtually every country in the world has a name for it and a different way of wearing and applying it. From Egypt to India, China to Spain, its magic has woven its way through history to become one of the true sacred plants.

The different names of henna used culturally include:

- Henu (*hnw*) or puker (Egyptian)
- Kupr or kufer (Coptic)
- Kypros (Greek)
- Kopfer (Jewish)
- Al-henna, hinna, al-qatab (Arabic)
- Mehndi (Hindi)
- Madayantika (Sanskrit)
- Egyptian privet, camphire, cypress shrub, Jamaica mignonette, smooth lawsonia (English)
- Alchanna (Medieval Latin, European)
- Quene (French)
- Wu bai zu, tche kia hoa (Chinese)
- Tsume hana (Japanese)

*Henna plant
(Lawsonia inermis)*

So Where Did It Come From?

It is often difficult to precisely pinpoint henna's origin due to continual migration and cultural integration, but there is evidence of its early use by the Egyptians, Jews, Greeks, Romans, Persians, and Indians. The ancient Egyptians used henna in the mummification process; the Romans reputedly took on the tradition of the Germanic Teutones to dye their hair flaming red when going to battle (traders accompanied them with supplies of henna); and the Romans documented the use of henna by the Jews in Jerusalem around the time of the birth of Christ. Some believe that henna was used during erotic rituals of the ancient goddess cultures of southern China.

> *The first thing that met his eyes was a*
> *mummified hand ... the long fingers were perfect,*
> *and the almond-shaped nails had been stained*
> *with henna, as was the embalmers' fashion.*
> —H. Rider Haggard, *Smith and the Pharaohs*

The earliest documented and proven uses of henna were discovered in the tombs of the ancient Egyptians. Several of the mummies discovered were found to have had their hands and feet stained or their hair pasted with what we presume is henna, indicating that this was perhaps a part of the mummification ritual. Dried henna leaves have also been found in Late Kingdom tombs. The nineteenth-century Egyptologist and botanist P. E. Newbury discovered some henna twigs at a Ptolemaic cemetery at Hawara, Egypt, which was recorded in the notes of fellow Egyptologist William Flinders Petrie.

There are several etchings on pyramid walls (c. 2291 BCE) that directly mention "henu"—henna. This is further substantiated by the use of the word *henu* in hieroglyphics found repeatedly throughout Egyptian history, and it is categorically

mentioned in some detail in the Ebers Papyrus, an ancient pharmacopoeia written in Thebes around 1500 BCE. The Egyptian word for henna in its consonant form was *hnw* or later in the Coptic form *Kpr*, translated as "Kupros" or "Cyperus."

The Egyptian origin of henna seems to be the most compelling, as there is so much documented evidence, but that may be due purely to the superb recordkeeping skills of the ancient Egyptians. Much has obviously been lost, but we do have sufficient evidence to prove that they used this wonderful plant in its medicinal and perfumery capacity and as a dye for their hair and fingernails.

> *My beloved is unto me as a*
> *cluster of camphire [henna flowers]*
> *in the vineyards of Engedi.*
> —The Song of Solomon 1:14

Henna is mentioned in the Bible, especially in the words of the Song of Solomon, where it is often referred to as "camphire," and also in the Babylonian Talmud, where it states that "the rose, henna, lotus, and balsam, as well as their proceeds, are subject to the laws of the sabbatical year."

· ·
What Was Henna Used For?

Henna has been used for centuries in various capacities:

Medicinal: A few examples are for cuts, stings, astringent, and cooling (as a sunscreen).

Cosmetic: Predominantly used as a hair dye but also to stain nails.

Decorative: Used as a skin decoration during special occasions and rituals or for pleasure.

Healing Henna

The naturalist Pliny and Greek physician Dioscorides both mention a tree called cyprus in their first-century AD writings; it derives from *kypros,* a name given to the henna that was found in abundance on the island of Cyprus. Cyprus grew at Canopus on the Egyptian Delta, and it has now been identified as being *Lawsonia inermis* (henna), as it had very fragrant flowers. Pliny mentions a recipe for Cyprinum unguent using the plant: "Take seeds of the cyprus tree and boil them in olive oil. Crush the seeds and strain the oil."

This ointment was described by Dioscorides as "sweet smelling, heating and mollifying," which mellowed the taste of "hot medicine" when ingested.[1] He also recommended henna for mouth ulcers and "hot inflammations and carbuncles," and suggested mixing the flowers with vinegar to apply to the forehead for headaches.

The Ebers Papyrus mentions seven types of henna, depending on the age of the plant or part of the plant used and where it was obtained (henna from the north, henna from the fields, henna from the marshes, etc.). Each area would produce a slightly different type or strength of henna due to the environmental conditions, such as aridity or moisture, which affected the lawsone (pigment) content of the plant. It is now known that water severely inhibits the staining quality of henna, and therefore it is understandable that cultivation of the plant was often restricted to hot, dry climates. To make full use of henna's depth of staining, it is imperative to obtain powder that has been dried and stored correctly. If the leaves were damp when they were collected, the chance of obtaining a good dark stain is less likely. However, using a henna paste from fresh leaves was a common practice for

---

1   Lise Manniche, *An Ancient Egyptian Herbal* (London: British Museum Publications Ltd., 1989), 54.

medicinal purposes as it did not leave a stain; therefore, treating a headache by plastering the paste on the forehead would leave the patient mercifully unstained.

Henna's medicinal uses in ancient Egypt ranged from treating fungal infections and inflammation to an astringent to stop diarrhea and as a cure for snake bites and scorpion stings. It was also used as a cooling remedy, often applied to the palms of the hands or soles of the feet, or as a form of deodorant by placing the leaves under the arms. Women from Nubia would use the plant to deepen the already dark qualities of their skin until they resembled "a ripe date."[2]

One quote from the Ebers Papyrus is a recommendation of the healing qualities of henna, taken from the temple of Osiris: "Look to it because this is the true remedy. It was found among the proven remedies in the temple of the God Osiris. It is a remedy, which drives away the scurf in every limb of a person. Yes, it heals at once. You see."[3]

Henna is still used in the beautiful Egyptian Kyphi recipe used for incense, oils, and unguents. Kyphi is revered as a highly spiritual mix and was traditionally used at night.

In Muslim societies, henna was also used extensively in a medicinal capacity; according to the recordings of Mohammad-Baqer Majlesi: "Allah safeguards against three [diseases] whoever dyes oneself with henna: *jodam* (true leprosy), *baras* (vitiligo), and *ākela* (chancre)."[4] The application of henna was believed to play a part in the traditional practices of the prophets, including hennaing the hair to cure headaches and applying it to help prevent body odor. In various *hadiths* (oral traditions) of Islam, the use of henna as a remedy or as a dye was mentioned; as

2   Ibid., 114.

3   Catherine Cartwright-Jones, The Henna Page, http://www.hennapage.com/henna/encyclopedia/medical/ebers.html.

4   Hušang 'Alam, "Henna," *Encyclopaedia Iranica Online* (vol. 12, 2004), www.iranica.com.

Hazrat Umme Salma narrated: "In the life of the Prophet Muhammad, no injury or thorn piercing was treated on which henna was not applied."[5]

These remedies and traditions have continued and are used in rural areas to this day through folklore recipes for cracked heels, knife wounds, ringworm, and scalp problems.

Use henna, it makes your head lustrous,
cleanses your hearts, increases the sexual vigour
and will be witness in your graves.
—Words from the Prophet Muhammad [6]

Henna, Hair, and Nails

Henna has been recorded as a dye for hair and nails since the ancient Egyptians documented it in their pharmaceutical and sacred papyri. As mentioned earlier, Egyptian mummies have been found that appear to have hennaed fingernails; some experts believe that this would have helped retain the lifelike appearance of the nails due to the conditioning properties of henna and also its ability to prevent fungal spores from growing on the body. The use of henna as a nail adornment is evident in Egypt from the New Kingdom period, but only on the hands of women in certain trades such as songstresses, entertainers, and prostitutes. It is likely that, similar to tattooing, the use of cosmetic henna in many ancient cultures may have been restricted to those of the lower classes.

5   As quoted in Dr. M. Laiq Ahmed Khan's article "Henna (Mehndi) Is a Great Healer," http://www.islamic voice.com/november.99/tibb.htm.
6   Ibid.

In later years, hennaed fingernails were seen in a variety of cultures such as the Kingdom of Lanna (Lan Na, or Kingdom of Million Rice Fields), a state in what is now northern Thailand from the thirteenth to eighteenth centuries, which has depictions of princesses with long hennaed nails and fingertips.

The use of henna to dye the hair (and even beards) was commonplace in many ancient cultures; the Egyptian King Ramses II is one of the most famous men to have hennaed hair, and it is possible that Queen Hatshepsut, the female pharaoh of the eighteenth dynasty, was also an advocate, as was her wet nurse, whose mummy still exhibits a swathe of deep auburn hair.[7]

Because the Prophet Muhammad documented his use of henna for dyeing his beard, his followers also adopted the practice, and it has been so until modern times. His daughter Fatima also applied henna to her hands, and the symbol of the Hand of Fatima is representative of her decorated palms.

Aside from wedding, birthing, and circumcision rituals, Muslims use henna to help celebrate various other very important festivals, such as the holy month of Ramadan, Eid al-Fitr, and Eid al-Adha.

Henna's wonderful conditioning and staining properties meant it was popular throughout Africa, India, and the Middle East, where it grew prolifically. Henna strengthens and binds keratin, which is the protein that makes up both hair and nails and so is perfect for keeping them strong, supple, and healthy. Due to its many medicinal properties, not only was henna a useful cosmetic, but it also helped maintain hair, skin, and nail health.

In the first century AD, the Greek physician Dioscorides mentions a henna "shampoo" for dyeing the hair yellow or reddish made from pulverized henna

7   See http://mathildasanthropologyblog.wordpress.com/2008/07/21/mummies-and-mummy-hair-from -ancient-egypt/.

leaves that had been macerated in soapwort; for a black dye, oak galls, ivy, and various other plants were used. It has also been used in Indian Ayurvedic medicine, amongst other things, as a scalp treatment for dandruff and hair loss, and as sacred oil for the crown chakra, which is the spiritual point on the top of the head that represents our communion with our higher nature or God.

Over the centuries, many women have stained their nails with henna for cosmetic and religious purposes. As hennaing does not prohibit water from cleansing the body, it was deemed to be suitable for Jewish and Muslim women to use.

The beauty of henna as a hair dye spread across the globe and was seen as the epitome of exotica when it reached the realm of the nineteenth-century Victorians. The lustrous, flaming chestnut or mahogany locks created by pure red henna were viewed as quite daring, and it was mainly actresses, ladies of the night, or bohemian society girls who flaunted them. Various other types of "henna" were also available, but they were not pure red henna but rather other herbs or plants with conditioning or staining properties to create a wealth of colours, some of which have now been proven to be potentially dangerous.

· ·

Henna's Sacred Art

Records show that the use of henna paste as a form of decoration or mystical symbolism has been in practice globally for around 5,000 years. According to some authorities, the earliest text mentioning henna in the context of fertility and marriage rituals derives from the Ugaritic legend of Baal and Anath. Ugarit was a prominent town in the ancient land of Syria around 2100 BCE; several fragments of clay tablets found there allude to a word assumed to mean "henna." In translation, the myth mentions that the goddess Anath would adorn herself with rouge and "henna" (or the word believed to mean henna) before slaughtering men and wading in their blood! There are also several statues and wall paintings from the Mediterranean circa 1700 BCE that imply the use of henna as a bodily decoration. However, there are several other plants that can produce a dye similar to henna, such as ochre, vermillion, sandalwood, and alkalized turmeric, and therefore we may be wrong to assume that all red body art has been created by henna.

For centuries, women have used henna culturally and ritually to enhance their sexuality, to celebrate, or to protect themselves or others. They hennaed their hands and feet to keep themselves safe from the evil eye, which could cause them to be infertile or bring about catastrophe for themselves or their families. Red palms have been associated with love and fertility for centuries; dancers, wives, and princesses all used the potent power of henna to protect, enhance, or seduce. They were hennaed for love, betrothal, marriage, pregnancy, childbirth, and health.

All over the world, henna has been used ceremonially for centuries, and even today it is still a major part of celebrations and rituals from different cultures. The Muslim festivals of Eid al-Fitr, Eid al-Adha, and Mawlid are all celebrated with the joyous application of henna to the women and children; during Eid al-Fitr, even the animals get hennaed! In the Hindu religion, the celebrations of Diwali and Karwa Chauth include henna, and Jews still incorporate it in the festivals of Purim and Passover. Marriages, births, deaths, and circumcision are also celebrated with henna decorations in Jewish, Hindu, and Muslim cultures. However, during the 1500s in Spain, henna came under persecution. In an edict issued in Granada in 1526 by the Roman Catholic Church, the decorating of fingernails with henna was banned due to the anti-Muslim and anti-Jewish movement. This was briefly overturned, only to be reinstated in 1530, whereby any woman found to be decorated with henna was brought before the Inquisition, and usually under torture she was questioned as to the nature of the use. If henna was found to be used for Muslim or Jewish celebrations, she would be convicted of heresy and put to death;

*A North African/Moroccan-style pattern
hennaed goatskin drum top (6-inch size)*

if it was proven to be merely for decoration, she was spared. Finally, in 1567, henna was banned completely. Luckily, this was not to be permanent, and today henna is freely available to use around the world.

Henna designs vary from region to region, with cultural influences vividly depicted in the patterns. There tend to be three main types of design that are commonly used:

Indian: These tend to be very intricate and almost like lace, with floral, paisley, and fine lines used.

Arabic: The designs tend to be based around nature and are often quite large, with flowers, leaves, and calligraphy interwoven.

African: These are bold, geometric, and made with a combination of thick and thin lines.

· ·

All-Purpose Henna

Not only has henna been used as a medicine, a cosmetic, and a human body art form, its incredible dyeing power has been used throughout the centuries to dye wool and silk and decorate drums, lamps, and other leather goods in general. Even animals have been dyed with henna. In Lebanon, Syria, and Palestine, springtime equinox festivals were held where the horses were decorated with henna, possibly dating back to around 2,000 BCE.[8] Horses would have their hooves, manes, and tails stained red for festivals and battles; beautiful patterns would be painted onto the animals that would unsettle the enemy and convey a powerful image of strength and victory.

8   The Henna Page, http://www.hennapage.com/henna/encyclopedia/horses/springfest.html.

Goats and sheep were also purified with henna for traditional feast days and sacrifice in Middle Eastern countries.

The beautiful poem "In Praise of Henna" is by the Indian politician and poet Sarojini Naidu (1879–1949):

> A kokila[9] called from a henna-spray:
> Lira! liree! Lira! liree!
> Hasten, maidens, hasten away
> To gather the leaves of the henna-tree.
> Send your pitchers afloat on the tide,
> Gather the leaves ere the dawn be old,
> Grind them in mortars of amber and gold,
> The fresh green leaves of the henna-tree.
>
> A kokila called from a henna-spray:
> Lira! liree! Lira! liree!
> Hasten maidens, hasten away
> To gather the leaves of the henna-tree.
> The tilka's red for the brow of a bride,
> And betel-nut's red for lips that are sweet;
> But, for lily-like fingers and feet,
> The red, the red of the henna-tree.[10]

9   An Indian cuckoo, a bird often mentioned in the Kama Sutra.

10 From *The Golden Threshold* by Sarojini Naidu. Project Gutenberg: http://www.gutenberg.org/ebooks/680.

Chapter 2

Magic

Magic: (1) the art that purports to control or forecast natural events, effects, or forces by invoking the supernatural; (2a) the practice of using charms, spells, or rituals to attempt to produce supernatural effects or control events in nature; (2b) the charms, spells, and rituals so used.[11]

• •

So What Is Magic?

The word *magic* comes from the Latin *magicus*, which in turn comes from the Greek *magikos*, which was in reference to the "magical" arts of the magicians, or magi, the Zoroastrian priests of ancient Persia.

Magic could be viewed as an unseen force that surrounds us all, a cosmic web of energy that is just waiting to be tapped into. You do not need to be of any one religion, class, or creed to make magic manifest in your life, and later in this book we will see just how much magic we already use in our everyday lives. Magic is everywhere!

11 From http://www.thefreedictionary.com/magic.

There are so many different definitions of magic floating around in the world, it would take about half the book to cover them, but to put it very, very simply, magic is the process of influencing events through spiritual force or energy, or the manipulation of energy to create a desired effect.

The Magical Basics

My first magical tutor used to say, "Magic is as magic does." (And no, I had no idea what she was talking about either … at first.) In a nutshell, she was demonstrating that magic is all about cause and effect. Still confused? Follow me …

When we want to create a magical effect, we need a bundle of things to make it happen. Scott Cunningham, probably one of the most famous writers on Paganism, once said that "to perform effective magic, three necessities must be present: the need, the emotion, and the knowledge."

My similar advice includes the following steps:

Intent: The desire to create change and also the belief that it will work.

Knowledge: Knowing what it is you wish to achieve and how to achieve it.

Creation: The way you create the change through a spell, ritual, or prayer using the appropriate methods.

Sounds simple? It is, but there are a few things you may want to know before you get started. Here are some rules that most practitioners of magic believe are the right way to go:

Ground Rule #1: Harm No Other

The intention of your spell, ritual, or prayer should be of sound morals—e.g., do nothing that would harm another creature.

Ground Rule #2: Avoid Outward Manipulation of Another's Will

The intention of your spell, ritual, or prayer ideally should not manipulate another into doing something that is against their beliefs or that is morally reprehensible.

Ground Rule #3: Keep Your Magic to Yourself

It is often best to avoid telling all and sundry what spell you have done. Aside from the fact that some people get very antsy over the word *magic*, talking about it can essentially dilute the energy and strength of the work.

. . . .
Can Anyone Do It?

Absolutely! Magic is not restricted to any particular religion or spiritual path. Many Christians, Jews, and nonsectarian people "do" magic as well as Witches, Pagans, and Wiccans. Magical energy is something that has been in our lives for millennia, and it certainly does not discriminate! The ancient Egyptians were firm believers in magic, or *heka*, as they called it; they had no concept of the supernatural—they firmly believed it was just natural, an everyday occurrence in their lives. So whether you believe in one god/dess, many god/desses, or no god/dess, you can draw upon the abundance of universal energy that is there for us. Isn't that great?

Magic is believing in yourself—
if you can do that, then anything can happen.
—Johann Wolfgang von Goethe

There are, of course, many different belief systems all over the world—not just the main four religions of Christianity, Buddhism, Judaism, and Islam, but myriad spiritual paths that permeate our separate cultures, each with their own way of doing things. So which one is right? Probably all of them! We have discovered over the centuries that almost all spiritual paths hold some wisdom in common, something that is often referred to as parallel or perennial thinking or tradition. More recently, we have found that many of the different belief systems from cultures scattered across the globe have very similar concepts, even though it is impossible that they could have passed on the earliest ancient traditions via oral transmission. So that shows that there is definitely a spiritual link between the collective human unconsciousness, which we still have to fathom a bit further but which is incredibly exciting!

- -

A Magical Web:
Weaving the Wisdom

Magic is not a practice. It is a living, breathing web of energy that,
with our permission, can encase our every action.
—Dorothy Morrison, *Everyday Magic*

Some people like to visualize magical energy as a kind of cosmic spider's web. This comes from the ancient Anglo-Saxon magician's concept of what they called the way or web of Wyrd. They believed that everything was interconnected, and whatever occurred on one level reverberated on another, rather like a shudder along one strand of a spider's web would make the rest of the web tremble. This is also seen in the Hermetic tradition that originated in ancient Egypt; followers of this spiritual path use the premise of "as above, so below," meaning that what happens on earth is reflected in heaven and vice versa, and that we should strive to make heaven on earth by living a moral and uncorrupted life. This all ties in with the ground rules of magic—that you use your magical skills for positive or creative change and not for negative, destructive chaos.

· ·

It's a Kind of Magic!

Did you know that many of the things we do in everyday life are well within the realms of magic?

How many of you have made a wish when you blew out the candles on your birthday cake? A little bit of candle magic performed on a very special day—your solar birthday!

Have you ever eaten a hot cross bun, an Easter egg, or Passover bread? These are great examples of magical food—incorporating a symbol/energy into something that you then ingest and digest throughout your whole being.

Hands up—who has saluted a solitary magpie to avoid bad luck or recited the poem "one for sorrow, two for joy, three for a girl, four for a boy, five for silver, six for gold, seven for a secret never to be told," meaning however many magpies you saw would bring you the associated item?

Many superstitions or folklore are what we would call sympathetic magic—magic based on imitation, using correspondences and/or items to represent the magical energy. A *correspondence* is something that is believed to influence something else based on its resemblance or relationship to it—the idea being that like affects like.

A simple example would be using a symbol to connect with the focus or energy of something—a picture of the moon would conjure aspects of the magical energy

that the moon represents, such as emotions, dreams, or femininity. Some traditions use physical objects such as wands, poppets (little dolls), or other fetishes to link with the energies; many use charms, mandalas, and other sacred artwork.

Sympathetic Magic

The idea of sympathetic magic dates back to prehistoric times, when drawing a scene on a cave wall of a successful hunt would put the hunters in a positive-belief frame of mind so they would go out and be triumphant in their quest. Magical thinking can often describe how we see the world when we are children—we do or say something in the belief that it may happen, but that is not to say that magical thinking is childish. It is a simplistic way of effecting either a mental or physical change. And this is how we will use a lot of the spells and charms for henna magic—by drawing a design to tap into the magical energy that is associated with the particular symbol. Later in this book, you will read about how henna designs have been used throughout history in all manner of ways to celebrate, protect, cleanse, and much more.

Making Magic:
The Mystical Melting Pot

Symbols

We use symbols for many things in our everyday life—on signs to instruct, warn, or guide us; on books, food packets, and leaflets to educate and enlighten us. Historical and religious buildings are often covered in symbols, and of course we also use them for bodily decoration such as jewelry, clothing, and tattoos. Each symbol has a meaning and draws our attention to what it is trying to tell us, linking in to our deep unconscious. In magical practices, the symbol combined with our intent creates a stronger association and makes the magic stronger.

Scents and Senses

Have you ever smelled a fragrance and been transported back to your childhood, to a treasured holiday destination, or had a specific perfume conjure a vivid image of a favourite auntie? I'm sure you've all smelled something that has made you instantly think YUCK as well! Well, that is also how our senses work in respect to magical work—a symbol, scent, or colour can link us immediately with a concept, persona, or place. It is a wonderful way of helping the mind to focus on the intent and desire while also creating a great atmosphere for magic. We will use essential oils and herbs in our henna recipes later in the book, along with other ideas for creating your perfect space for spells and magic, such as making it into a ritual.

Amulets, Charms, and Talismans

People have been using amulets, charms, and talismans since the dawn of time—so what's the difference?

Amulet: An object with an intrinsic power of protection, believed to absorb negative qualities and protect the wearer. Examples of traditional amulets are crosses, ancient Egyptian symbols such as the ankh or Eye of Horus, or other deity-related symbols.

Charm: An object (or words) constructed or enhanced with the magical power to enchant; usually a magic spell is cast to make a statue, piece of jewelry, or other object have an effect on others and may make it behave in a way that it shouldn't. The Harry Potter books are filled with charms for making broomsticks misbehave, cars fly, and hats talk!

Talisman: An object made with a specific intent—they effectively act as a generator of energy to achieve a specific goal. Talismans are made specifically for the wearer, often incorporating elaborate designs of magical correspondences such as angelic, elemental, or planetary sigils to empower the intended result.

What Is Ritual, and Why Do We Do It?

Ritual is described in the *Oxford Popular English Dictionary* as "a series of actions used in a religious or other ceremony." Rituals can be performed at various special times dictated by tradition or a religious holiday, in a group, by an individual, or by a whole community. It can be done inside, outside, in public or private; in fact, anywhere the need takes it (within reason, obviously)—that is the beauty of doing a ritual! Some examples of rituals that we see around us all the time are:

Cultural traditions: Christmas, Halloween, Thanksgiving, Easter, Diwali, Ramadan, Chinese New Year.

Religious services: A very obvious and simple way of demonstrating faith and the components or traditions of that faith.

Rites of passage: Presidential inaugurations, graduations, marriages, bar mitzvahs, confirmations, funerals, dedication ceremonies, coronations.

These are all rituals, as they follow a set format that is symbolic yet confers certain energy, whether it is of a spiritual or more physical type.

As the nature of ritual is symbolic, that means there are hardly any limits to the actions, or "ingredients," that can be used:

- Gestures, words, song, dance, music, costume...
- Food, drink, plants, herbs, oils...
- Objects such as candles, feathers, stones, mirrors...

The list is almost endless and gives you great scope for making your own very special ceremony. So ritual is a wonderful way of making your magic more potent and real. It also allows you to put due care and thought into what it is that you require or need—and that is where the next bit comes in.

Correspondences: What Are They, Which Do I Use, and When Do I Use Them?

Since the student is a man surrounded by material objects, if it be his wish to master one particular idea, he must make every material object about him directly suggest that idea. Thus in the ritual quoted, if his glance fall upon the lights, their number suggests Mercury; he smells the perfumes, and again Mercury is brought to his mind. In other words, the whole magical apparatus and ritual is a complex system of mnemonics.
—Aleister Crowley, *Liber O*

Correspondences are objects, beings, or concepts that are thought to be linked through magical or supernatural means, as already explained in the passage about sympathetic magic. Often they are shown as a table of correspondences, which is effectively a list showing how all the items or ideas fit together, and they are really useful tools when creating magical spells and rituals. All these things help

to create a link with our chosen desire; once we are aware of the connections between the correspondences, it produces a profound effect on our thoughts and senses. Correspondences can include symbols, elements, angels, planets, colours, astrological signs, numbers, days of the week, plants, oils, herbs, gemstones, and deities; also included are the negative and positive mental, physical, and spiritual attributes.

Let's use the planet Mars as an example of how all those things can be joined in some way and used for magical work.

MARS

Colour: Red

Astrological signs: Aries, Scorpio

Numbers: 2, 3, 5, 16

Day of week: Tuesday

Element: Fire

Metals: Iron, steel

Minerals: Jasper, garnet, ruby, bloodstone

Gods: Horus, Ares, Heracles, Mars

Goddesses: Brigit, Anath, Morrigen

Angel: Samael

Tarot card: The Tower

Herbs/plants: Garlic, ginger, tobacco, pine, basil, asofoetida

Oils: Pine, pepper, ginger, galangal

Qualities: Power, protection, strength, energy, ambition, victory, motivation, medical issues, lust, anger, war, conflict, upheaval, destruction...

Useful for: Promoting courage; physical, mental, and spiritual strength; sexual energy; protection during surgery and for postoperative healing; protective magic; banishing others' negative energies; and so on...

As you can see, there are endless ways that you can mix and match the different correspondences to use for your spells. You do not need to use them all; you can just decide you need Mars energy for your spell to help you get that job, and then add two red candles, some pine incense, call on one of the god/desses or angels for help, and do your spell on a Tuesday using a symbol associated with your aim. Voilà!

Chapter 3

Henna Magic Through the Ages

She loved him then, she loved him now
She met him in a dream some way, somehow,
He is hers as she is his, their destiny had already been written
This henna on her hands tells her so,
In her hands his heart is gently rocked to and fro.
—Anonymous

. . . .

Henna's Journey

Although henna was predominantly used in ancient times as a medicine, it later emerged as a highly important part of various cultures' celebrations, rites of passage, and protection rituals.

Each country has a different way of preparing and using dried henna, and there are myriad recipes for mixing the paste and applying it to the skin. The dried and crushed leaves can be mixed with other herbs, oils, and spices to create different hues and permanence. Black tea, coffee, cloves, indigo, lemon juice, eucalyptus, and tea tree oil are some of the familiar ingredients used.

The art form itself also varies from region to region, with each culture having differing depictions of symbols and tracery. Many of the practices overlap to some extent, but each religion or tribe has its own distinct way of applying henna for the resulting designs.

However, a key element in all of the sacred body art is that somewhere within it is a conscious or unconscious magical belief. Most of the designs protect, repel, entice, or include specific symbols to connect with a certain energy or goal—a perfect example of sympathetic magic. The skin becomes a living charm, amulet, or talisman and allows the energy of the person to flow through it, thereby creating a powerful and beautiful current.

And so henna has been used to accompany people throughout the many rites of passage in their lives, bringing colour and vitality into the occasion or functioning as a comforting (or stark) reminder of the path to be followed.

· ·

Henna in India

In India, the name of henna for skin decoration is traditionally known as mehndi, and its most common use is for festivals and special occasions such as weddings, births, funerals, and so on. It is a very important part of Indian life and is considered to be very lucky; adornment of brides' hands and feet is almost mandatory. Mehndi incorporates intricate, lacy, floral, or paisley designs covering the hands, feet, arms, and shins; sometimes the back or chest is also decorated. The designs also incorporate spiritual or religious aspects, although the overall result is often abstract. In Indian culture, women have always been encouraged to pay particular attention to their bodies and beauty. The Kama Sutra gives clear instructions as to how they should make themselves alluring to men—amongst other things, they were taught how to tattoo themselves with henna and to stain their nails and

teeth! It also mentions that a woman makes the transition from virgin to seductress when adorned with henna before her wedding.

When an Indian girl has her first menstrual period, the women celebrate her transition from child to woman with her first henna application, and she is then taught the "art of love" in preparation for her future marriage. Mehndi is listed within the Kama Sutra as one of the sixty-four arts for women, and the darker the stain and the more elaborate the design is said to be an indication of how well the young woman has been instructed in the art of love. Basically, if the design took a long time, her erotic lessons would have been more in-depth!

Henna artists in India are traditionally a part of the Nai, or Barber caste, and the practice is passed down through the generations. Many artists are also women who are unable to work outside the home, who offer exquisite handiwork for brides and festivalgoers, of which there are many, for every joyous occasion is usually accompanied by henna applications.

· ·

Henna in Africa, the Middle East, and Islam

Henna became part of the Islamic culture in or around the sixth and seventh centuries AD and spread throughout the Middle East along with the religion. As Islam forbids the use of human representation in art or decoration, the use of images bearing human faces or those of animals or birds are disallowed. So most Middle Eastern designs tend to be more abstract and less dense, featuring graceful floral and vine patterns, similar to those found in Arabic art and tile/textile designs. These are much less complex than the mehndi designs used in India. Henna is much used even to this day for the Muslim religious festivals, particularly Eid al-Adha, the Feast of Sacrifice.

Henna was first used in Morocco with the migration of the Berbers to the region, most likely from Yemen. When the Arabs invaded during the eighth century, they added the rich Berber culture to their own. Because Islam forbids the use of tattoos, women learned to use henna as a means of decoration. The designs were employed for ritual use to help protect against the evil eye and also for traditional celebrations such as weddings, births, and funerals. Traditional Berber and Moroccan designs are usually made up of bold geometric shapes, eyes, plants, and flowers, and they are undeniably beautiful in their uniqueness, full of magical symbolism. The number five is symbolic in both the Jewish and Islamic traditions and is often depicted as a hand known as a *khamsa* (*hamsa*, *hamesh*, or *chamsa*), meaning "five" in Hebrew; it is more commonly recognized as the Hand of Fatima or Hand of Miriam. The numeric symbolism is illustrated by the five digits of the hand, which in turn can remind us of the five pillars of Islam; Heh, the fifth letter of the Hebrew alphabet and part of the holy name of God; and also the five books of the Jewish Torah. This design is seen all over the Middle East on jewelry or wall hangings, or painted on the walls, and it is believed to be a powerful defence against the evil eye (see chapter 4).

Most of the henna designs were created as charms for fertility and protection of all kinds, made up of triangular, star, or diamond shapes; these angular, geometric motifs were designed to repel negative forces by their sharp contours. One of the most simple yet powerful designs is of an eye within a heart, which is believed to protect your beloved from the covetous looks or advances of others.

Khamsa patterns

Khamsa patterns

Henna in Jewish Cultures

The documented use of henna by Jews is found in writings by the Romans. There is also some reference to the painting of hands with henna as far back as Old Testament times. Sephardic Jews used henna as decoration for their celebrations as far back as 1000 BCE. Kurdish Jews used henna in their social and religious celebrations as recently as the twentieth century.

Henna Rituals in History and Beyond

Pregnancy and Childbirth

Pregnancy and childbirth were seen as two very important times when the mother and child needed as much protection and blessings as possible. It was seen as a precarious time, as it was believed in many cultures that evil spirits lurked where there was the promise of pure new life and the spilling of blood. In most of the Middle Eastern, Asian, and North African lands, traditional rituals and celebrations would accompany both the late stages of pregnancy and the process of childbirth. All of them reflect the use of sympathetic magic—using symbols, charms, spells, or talismans that bring about a positive and protective result.

In India, the eighth month of pregnancy is deemed particularly auspicious, and the *athawansa* ceremony is performed. On the first day of her eighth month, the mother-to-be is ritually bathed using perfumed water, and then she has mehndi applied to her feet and hands, similar to that of her wedding day. She is then richly dressed, sat on a ceremonial seat, and piled high with trinkets, sweets, and a coconut, which is a traditional part of the ritual, called "the filling of the lap." The whole ceremony is designed to help the woman feel protected and firmly part of the community.

In Morocco and areas where the Berber people (or Amazigh) lived, before the actual birth, women would be decorated as if they were once again a bride, with henna, kohl, and a lip stain made from crushed walnut root. This was predominantly for protection, but as there was always a risk of death while giving birth, she was also prepared to be received as a bride in paradise. The area around the birthing room would also be ritually prepared by the midwife and attending women. A circle of protection would be drawn around the mother-to-be with a sword, and amulets, talismans, and incense would be placed around the room. The laboring woman would be hennaed with protective symbols to repel djinn, or malicious spirits. The Berber woman would be covered while giving birth so that evil could not see her and attempt to harm her or the baby. In India, after the birth, the woman is hennaed immediately on her finger- and toenails; this ceremony is called *jalva pujani* and is a ritual to purge the mother of anything negative or impure left over from the delivery of the baby. This is considered a dangerous time for both mother and child, as they need to be protected from malicious spirits and recover from the birthing process.

After the birth, it was common for the mother and child to be kept secluded from the world, surrounded only by her female relatives and the midwife. Seven to ten days later, depending on the culture, a naming ceremony would be held, and the child would be hennaed. In India, the baby would be decorated with solar symbols and held up to the sky to ask for the blessings of the life-giving, nurturing, and protective sun gods. It was symbolic of the child's appearance into the world and of the mother's new role and integration back into the life of the village community. Even after the seventh- or tenth-day celebration, the festivities continued as long as the family could afford them; female relatives would help with the running of the household while the new mother continued to rest and spend time with her baby, and this often involved more lengthy sessions of henna

application, which required her to be still for several hours. She was also dismissed from household chores to allow the henna to retain its stain for as long as possible; again, this ensured adequate rest and relaxation for the mother for up to forty days after the birth. This time of transition was not only for ritual and traditional purposes but also to give the woman a chance to recuperate fully both physically and mentally, thus reducing the incidence of postpartum illness or depression.

In Morocco, multiple births were classed as particularly auspicious, and the mother was deemed to be incredibly blessed. When the baby was born, the umbilicus would be cut, the end dabbed with henna and ritually disposed of by the midwife. All these protective rituals were comforting to the mother, for she knew that she had been surrounded and protected by people she could trust and that they had done all they could to make sure the birth was as safe as possible. The newborn baby would also be protected from the evil eye by the application of henna, either by dabbing it on their face and hands or via a henna rub consisting of henna mixed with oil or butter that was then massaged all over the baby. This was often applied for the first seven days in place of washing. However, recently it has been discovered that applying henna to infants can be dangerous, as it may expose the child to a rare but possibly fatal blood disorder.

Circumcision

Boys in the Berber families were not circumcised at birth but rather at the age of four during a family celebration. It was an important and costly affair, and the family would save up for some time to prepare for the circumcision party; there was a sacrificial sheep and a fine suit of clothes for the boy to buy. All the relatives would be invited, fed, and given a gift, and if an eminent family was holding the party, the entire village would be in attendance. The day before the ritual, the women of the family would gather to watch the barber shave the boy's head. He would leave little tufts of hair, which the women would pay the boy to cut off, all

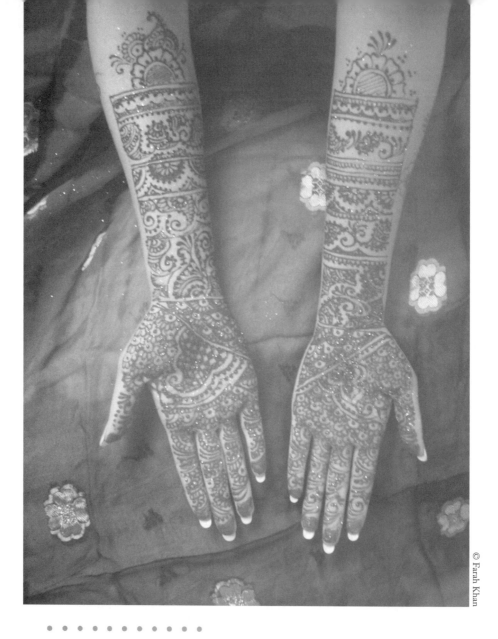

Modern mehndi

the time trilling and ululating as each piece was neatly removed. Afterwards, they would henna the boy's hands just the same as if he were a bride. The following morning, his family would take him to the "wedding spring," called the Tamusi, which is where brides would also be taken prior to their wedding. Here, the boy would be bathed like a bride-to-be before being taken back home for his circumcision. He would appear hennaed and painted, dressed beautifully, and maybe even laid out on a bed like a bride, awaiting his ceremony, whereby he would be admonished to be brave and not to cry during the circumcision. He would be held still while the barber or other experienced authority performed the operation with a sharp knife. The women trill as the skin is removed and the wound covered with henna and a clean bandage. The feast would then commence, followed by much celebration.

Weddings

Henna has long played a part in the beautiful celebrations of marriage held in the Middle East, India, and Africa. In India, weddings are elaborate affairs considered to be one of the most sacred rituals; the celebrations often go on for days before and after the ceremony, with henna playing a huge part. The Hindu pre-wedding ritual of the *mehndi raat* is one of the most important and involves a fun evening of eating, dancing, and of course henna, attended mostly by friends and relatives of the bride. The actual ritual varies from region to region and is dependent on the financial status of the bride's family, but on the whole it is a vibrant gathering to bless and celebrate the forthcoming marriage.

The mehndi party is usually held a few days before or on the eve of the actual wedding at the bride's home or other venue. If no relative is proficient in henna art, a professional mehndi artist is hired to apply the designs to the bride's hands and feet and perhaps smaller ones on the guests. In some areas, it is deemed auspicious for the mother or the sister-in-law of the bride to apply the first motif. The design

is believed to ritualistically transform the bride-to-be from her state of virginity to that of a loving wife for her husband. Popular designs are flowers, fruits, paisley, peacocks, vines, and shells; a common practice is one of hiding the bridegroom's name somewhere in the pattern, which he then must be clever enough to find! Sometimes the mehndi party is held at the traditional *sangeet* (a big pre-wedding party for bride, groom, or both), which involves lots of lighthearted banter, singing, and dancing. Before henna was introduced to India, brides would use turmeric, which produced a yellow stain. The spice would be daubed on arms, legs, and head, and then rolled all over her to give a golden glow.

After the mehndi ritual, it is customary that the bride-to-be does not leave her house until it is time for the wedding. During that time, her henna design is observed to see how dark the stain has become; according to tradition, the deeper the colour, the more her husband and in-laws will love her. The length of time the design lasts is also an auspicious sign and is regarded as a good omen that her marriage will be strong.

Weddings in Morocco are similar to those in India; the ceremonies start prior to the actual wedding and include much partying and hennaing. Men are included, and it is the perfect time for a mixture of tradition and serious celebration. The groom's party starts with his mother presenting him with a gift of henna, an egg, and some water. The egg is broken into the henna paste, and his hands are covered while four candles are lit and placed in the bowl, which is then balanced precariously on the head of his male friends as they dance around the room until is eventually falls and smashes on the floor. Meanwhile, over at the bride's house, she is dressed in a beautiful ensemble and sits in a throne, where she will spend the evening being pampered and hennaed. Her guests will entertain her by dancing, singing, and offering blessings while the traditional protective patterns of diamonds, triangles, and crosses are applied to her skin.

In the United Arab Emirates, weddings are often very elaborate and costly, with much preparation going towards the ceremony and the preceding rituals. It is not uncommon for the bride to spend forty days in seclusion before the wedding; during this time, she will be showered with gifts from her husband-to-be, including perfume and expensive silks and jewels. The week before the actual wedding ceremony, traditional parties are held with much dancing, singing, music, and henna. The bride's mehndi will be applied during her *laylat al-henna* ("night of the henna"), where she is also pampered and massaged with oils and perfume. Mehndi is applied to her feet and hands, and her hair is ritually washed. She is accompanied by her female friends and relatives, who sing, dance, and prepare delicious food to feast upon.

Modern Arabic henna

The Turkish Night of the Henna is once again similar to others with a party, music, and dancing. The bride would leave her guests, and henna would be brought to her on a tray with candles placed in the paste. Her future mother-in-law would thickly henna her right hand, then the left, and then press a gold coin into the paste. The other guests would then do the same. The bride's hands would be wrapped with the coins firmly in the henna and silk bags slipped over the wrappings. Her feet would then be hennaed in the same way, after which all the guests would join her once more for much raucous dancing and singing.

Often we only associate henna with the Indian or Middle Eastern countries mentioned previously, but its use is equally popular amongst Jewish people. The initial Jewish festivities in anticipation of a wedding begin with a betrothal party. The marriage would have been arranged by the families of the prospective bride and groom, and once the agreement is successful, they would arrange for a *qadoshe*, or betrothal. The day before the celebration, the family of the groom prepares a feast and delivers it to the girl's house. The following day, the groom is led in a procession to her home, and she is brought to him and unveiled so that he and all the guests can see that he is being given the right girl. He then kisses her hand, gives her a betrothal ring, and then smashes a wine glass on the floor to seal the deal. He then leaves to celebrate with his friends while the bride's hair, feet, and hands are hennaed and her friends dance and sing.

In addition to the qadoshe, there would also be the Night of the Henna (*lel hanna*) and, intriguingly, the False Night of the Henna. Both of these celebrations precede the wedding and involve much henna, food, and dancing.

The False Night of the Henna was actually a diversionary tactic to fool evil spirits into thinking that it was the *real* Night of the Henna. Because people believed that demons would come to a wedding and bring misfortune, infertility, and disas-

ter to the marriage, it would be held on the Thursday before the wedding, and the real Night of the Henna would be held at the close of the Sabbath.

The real Night of the Henna was a fabulous affair, and although it varied from family to family, the essence was the same: celebrating and hennaing well into the night. The bride and groom would have separate parties (similar to our Western traditions of stag and hen nights) and then often meet up for an extended feast involving both families' friends and relatives. First thing in the morning, women would bring henna to the groom's house and mix it in large bowls and leave it to stand until the evening. When it was time for the parties to begin, the mixed henna would be carried by several of the groom's relatives over to the bride's house in a ceremonial procession. Musicians would follow them, and the people would sing, "The henna is coming, the henna is coming!" while children attempted to grab the bowls from the carriers. Once the henna arrived, the evening would start by the hennaing of a bridal decoy, a young girl who would fool the evil eye into thinking she was the bride. Instead of focusing their malevolence on the bride, the djinn (or spirits) would mistakenly attack the girl, who would naturally be protected by the henna and could lure them away from the wedding party. The child would sit on the bride's lap all the while the bride was being hennaed; first, her hair was hennaed to give it a lustrous, glossy colour and shine, and then her right hand and left foot, and then vice versa, each pattern wrapped to protect it. A bowl of the henna would then be taken to the groom's house while the rest of the bride's guests and relatives would feast and dance and receive their own henna.

The groom's Night of the Henna would be similar to his betrothed's. A young boy would act as decoy for the evil eye and would sit on the groom's lap while he was hennaed in the same way as the bride, except his side and forelocks were hennaed. Once the hand and feet designs were dried, they were wrapped in linen. Later that night, the groom's party would make a procession to the bride's house,

where the celebrations and feasting would continue. Eventually the bride and groom would sleep, still with their henna wrappings on, while their families and friends stayed up to keep them protected until their wedding day.

Within the small Jewish Yemeni culture, the prenuptial ceremony is called *hinne* and is similar to other Sephardic Jewish henna rituals that represent the passage of transition for the bride-to-be from daughter to wife. About a week before the wedding, a huge party is thrown for the bride and her female friends and relatives that involves three processions, all involving a change of dress for the bride. Her clothes are amazingly elaborate and include layers of heavy jewelry that in total can weigh around ten kilograms (twenty-two pounds) and is symbolic of the burden that the bride takes on when she gets married. A headdress completes the ensemble, complete with flowers and herbs to repel the evil eye, and the young girl then begins the *zaffeh* procession. Her relatives and friends carry baskets of flowers and candles to light her way, and a mournful *hinne* song is sung about the painful separation of the bride from her family and childhood home. Then the procession breaks into spontaneous dancing, after which another costume change and dance takes place, and then the final procession. After one more change of clothes, the bride then processes to the stage for her henna ritual accompanied by her mother, who carries a basket containing dry henna. Her grandmother then adds water to make a paste, and all her family come and dab their finger into the henna, pressing it into the palm of the young bride and offering her a blessing—"May your life be filled with Torah! Good health, happiness, and love!" The evening then commences with more dancing and singing.

A fascinating article on the Jewish henna ceremony is found on the website jewishtreats.org, including the following excerpt:

> *According to tradition, the henna ceremony is a way of preparing the bride for*
> *her departure from her family, and the henna, pronounced in Hebrew* chenah,

represents the three mitzvot specifically connected to women: Challah (separating the challah), Nida (family purity) and Hadlakat Nayrot (lighting Shabbat candles).

Henna, the plant, is mentioned several times in the Bible. In particular, Rashi (Rabbi Shlomo ben Yitzchak, France, eleventh century) commented that clusters of henna flowers are a metaphor for forgiveness and absolution, showing that God forgave those who tested Him in the wilderness. So too the bride and groom are given a clean slate with which to begin their lives together.

Death and Funerals

In some regions of Kurdistan, the death of a young man or woman would often prompt the use of henna for adorning the body. If they were unmarried, they would be dressed and decorated as if for their wedding, which would afford them joy in the afterlife. Songs would be sung, and if the young person had been engaged, their bride- or groom-to-be would come, and wedding rings would be symbolically exchanged. Henna would not be worn by the female relatives for a year after the death of a young man as they observed an official mourning period.

There are, however, some slightly darker uses for mehndi, one of which is for the decoration of widows who wish to partake in the ancient tradition of *sati* (suttee), whereby they voluntarily—or, in some cases, are forced to—burn themselves on their husband's funeral pyre. Often the same practice would occur if the women lost their men in battle; they would join them rather than become widows. Sati means "virtuous woman," and historically those who took part in the ritual would be revered as goddesses and believed to ascend directly to heaven. Rajput women would traditionally leave henna handprints on the walls of their house before immolation and often dressed and decorated themselves as they had been on their wedding day. This arcane ritual has been officially banned in India since 1829, but there have been cases as recently as 2008.

War

Henna has long been associated with war. The earliest reference was to the Uga-ritic fertility goddess Anath, the virgin warrior who used to henna her hands in celebration of the harvest and the victory over her enemies. There are several accounts of men being hennaed before going into battle—East Indian warriors, Kashmiri martyrs, and Iranian generals all used henna to some degree. The warriors would dip their hands in henna to remind them of their wives and loved ones at home; the Kashmiri men would be sent off to their deaths with hands hennaed by their mothers to fight the holy war. It is possible that the ancient Roman legionnaires used henna to paint their faces in an attempt to terrify their enemies, whereas the Teutonic tribes would dye their hair a flaming red using a mixture of animal fat, ashes, and henna. Catherine Cartwright-Jones mentions the use of henna by the Afghan fighters in the nineteenth century who "earned" their right to henna their fingernails when they had killed enough enemies; their leader described the practice to a traveler of the time as being similar to when "the falcon dips its talons in the blood of its prey."[12]

It was not just the soldiers that were hennaed in times of war. Often their horses received some henna, with their manes, tails, hooves, legs, and flanks dyed and decorated with striking designs.

12 From http://www.hennapage.com/henna/encyclopedia/war/talons.html.

Festivals

Karwa Chauth

This traditionally important Indian festival is designed for married women to dedicate the entire day in honor of their husbands and to wish them long life and prosperity. It is a time of fasting to show their devotion, which is then rewarded with fine gifts from both the husband and his family. The rituals begin the day prior to the festival with the mother-in-law giving the wife *sargi*, which can consist of sweets, clothes, and henna. The application of the henna is an integral part of the festival, not only for good luck but, similar to the wedding mehndi, for the belief that the darker the stain, the more the woman is loved and cherished by her husband.

Ramadan and Eid al-Fitr

Ramadan is the Islamic month of fasting and abstaining from sexual and social pleasures (e.g., smoking) during the period of sunrise to sunset. During Ramadan, Muslims concentrate heavily on their spiritual life, and prayer, charity, and atonement is vitally important, which spans from the first sighting of the crescent moon until the following crescent moon. It is similar to the Christian tradition of Lent, which involves fasting for the weeks before Easter. The Muslim women traditionally forego the use of cosmetics and other external beauty aids, and so when the end of Ramadan is in sight, they begin to prepare their return to their usual routines with the appreciation of a month's deprivation! The month of fasting ends with Eid al-Fitr (the festival to break the fast), a celebration in comparative importance to the Western Christmas or New Year. This festival lasts for three days. Eid is celebrated to thank Allah for past and future blessings received and is a time when everyone gets dressed up, enjoys festive food, and rejoices.

The women use henna to decorate and beautify themselves, and it is often a time to schedule weddings; almost everyone would have a little bit of henna—maybe just a simple design or a finger dipped in the paste. Some people would even henna their animal's tails, paws, or ears—dogs, horses, donkeys, and goats would be adorned, much to the delight of the children.

Eid al-Adha

The Festival of Sacrifice is celebrated by Muslims to commemorate Ibrahim's willingness to sacrifice his son Ismael as an act of obedience to Allah; God then provided a ram in place of Ismael. The festival is celebrated at the end of the yearly pilgrimage, or *hajj*, and used to coincide with the new growth of the henna plant in spring. Eid al-Adha traditionally involves dressing in the finest clothing and choosing a suitable domestic animal to sacrifice so that meat may be provided to all in the community. If situations do not allow for a sacrificial feast, money may be donated to ensure that food can be bought and distributed. In Islamic countries, the sacrificial animal was hennaed by the women as if it were a bride. Its hooves, tail, and head would be annointed with henna, and sometimes even a mouthful of paste was offered before the animal's throat was slit. For Eid al-Adha, everyone got hennaed; men, women, children, animals, and even the houses are given a decorative daub before the festivities begin in earnest.

Purim

Purim is a holiday celebrated by Jews to mark the rescue of the Jewish people by Queen Esther, the wife of a Persian king, from a plot to kill them. Until the early twentieth century, Kurdish girls would be ritually bathed, hennaed, and dressed to try and emulate Esther's beautification before she was presented to the king. Now, Purim is celebrated with colourful plays, readings from the Book of Esther, and joyous feasting, with sweets and gifts given to children and charity.

Henna for Animals

In Lebanon, springtime festivals were a traditional occurrence held in the six weeks before Eastern Orthodox Easter. They were held on successive Thursdays and attended by Christians, Jews, and Muslims, and during two of the festivals it was the animals that received decoration with henna. During the "Thursday of all the animals," domestic and farmed livestock would effectively have a day off from work and be brought to the festival to mate and "go forth and multiply"—the owners would henna the animals' foreheads as a blessing and to celebrate life. The last Thursday before Easter saw the gathering of several thousand people at the Shrine of Wali Zaur to receive blessings of fertility, health, and good fortune. Horses and donkeys were decorated with the blue "horse beads" of protection and bright garlands; the beautiful Arabian horses would have their tails dyed with henna, creating a swathe of vibrant red and orange.

A hennaed horse

Henna and the Djinn

Protection and Attraction

Throughout the Middle Eastern countries, the concept of the djinn has played a powerful part in their mythology, religious, and social practice, and a very common use for henna was to either placate or repel djinn.

Predating Islam, djinn were believed to be a race of entities that were part human, part fire—similar to the concept of elementals in the Western tradition. Just as God created man from clay, rendering him half man, half earth, the djinn were created before man from smokeless (or purest) fire. They are believed to be male or female, with the capacity to breed and also shapeshift. They are directly under God's will and live in a parallel existence to humans, enjoying a social, sexual, and spiritual life, but will still be called to Judgment. In Morocco, the djinn are classified elementally, being linked to earth, air, fire, or water, and often represented by flowers or colours; in some traditions, they are attributed to the number seven and the days of the week.

Like our concept of ghosts, most djinn are predominantly invisible, but they do have a direct relationship with humankind whereby they can be manipulated or coerced into doing the will of the human, often submitting to their invocations and bribes. They can equally be benevolent or malevolent, depending on their inclination—bringing chaos and pestilence or good fortune and health in equal measure. Benevolent and helpful djinn are attracted to all things beautiful and fragrant, and in particular they like henna; when pleased, they happily bestow favors and blessings. Malevolent djinn are renowned to live wherever disease, bodily fluids, blood, or excrement are prevalent, often near rubbish heaps or cemeteries. Pregnant or menstruating women are believed to be particularly at risk from their influence, as are newborn babies. Jealous of the ability of women to get

pregnant, give birth, and nurse their infants, the djinn often became incensed and consequently are a threat to both mother and baby. It is believed djinn can enter a woman via her menstrual blood, causing the kind of outbursts of anger, pain, and misery that we now call PMS.

There are a few djinn who are well known in Moroccan legend. Aisha Kandisha, a water djinn, is a particularly voracious spirit who would entrance both men and women, causing them to become so intoxicated by her that they were often driven to the brink of madness. Even today, it is not uncommon for people to be exorcised for possession by djinn, and there have always been special rituals involving the use of henna to rid the possessed of the evil influence. Women were perceived as the best intermediary between humans and djinn, and went through enormous preparation to protect themselves while they undertook the exorcism; they would ritually bathe, dress, and be hennaed in preparation.

If a woman was suffering from mental or physical imbalance or infertility, or was generally unwell, she could ask a medium to intervene or she could take part in a banishing ceremony to remove any malevolent influence. One of these rituals is known as *zar* and is still practiced in many Middle Eastern countries, either to banish negative spirits or influences or to allow communion with the gods or benevolent spirits. Believed to have originated in Ethiopia and brought to Egypt, the zar is a trancelike experience involving dance and a simple hypnotic music beat. Normally it is only practiced by women; modernly, it is seen as ridiculous by most men and is positively frowned upon by Islam. However, it is an important way for women to gather together and let off steam from their lives in a predominantly patriarchal society.

Similar ceremonies take place in Morocco, often in the form of henna parties, where there is much trance dancing and hennaing to dispel or placate malevolent djinn or, alternatively, to invite benevolent ones to gather. Parties might be

held prior to Ramadan—the application of henna would help protect them while they fasted, when they were believed to be more vulnerable to the attention of evil djinn—or simply as a gathering to protect a mother-to-be or new mother and baby.

It is well known that good djinn are attracted to henna, and there is even a henna djinn called Malika, who apparently particularly favors star and floral patterns and loves music, flowers, and the colours blue, mauve, and yellow. She is reputed to bring great joy, love, and happiness into your life, which is certainly a very good reason to invite the henna djinn into your house!

Children are often affected by the tricks and perils of djinn, and many mothers have used simple henna magic to keep the djinn from their doors. If a child was scared of something unseen or became very sick, it was assumed djinn were to blame; in Palestine, a mixture of salt, barley, sugar, and henna would be used to bribe the djinn to cease its devilry. The mix would be made into little pouches, and

A floral henna design

for three consecutive nights, one would be put under the child's pillow, named for the child, the disease, and the cause of the illness, respectively. The pouches would then be thrown one by one down a well (a place where djinn often dwell), and a short petition to the spirit would be recited to ask that good health be returned to the child. Another method would be to scatter the mix in the child's room and ask the djinn to take the barley to feed their animal, the sugar to treat their children, and the henna to decorate with, and in return the spirit should leave the child and household alone.

Another prudent exercise if you were visiting a house in Morocco and carrying henna was to leave a small amount for the household djinn—throwing a pinch in the fire or on the floor was usually sufficient to appease the spirits. To leave without making an offering was believed to be disrespectful and dangerous, and could lead to the djinn endangering or even killing a member of the household—or, if the guest had not told their host that they had henna, the djinn would attack the guest instead!

Modernly, the djinn and their antics are generally thought of as the equivalent of our fairy tales, but secretly many people still continue with offerings and prayers, just as Westerners still adhere to old superstitions such as touching wood or avoiding going under ladders.

. . . .

Purification

A Trip to the Hammam

The *hammam* (Turkish or public baths) was the place where women could gather socially to bathe, be massaged, and apply henna to each other. It was a segregated experience and a peaceful respite from the world of men; children of both sexes

were permitted to be with the women, but that was forbidden to the boys once they reached a certain age. A day at the hammam was a special event for the majority of women, and as they were obliged to attend due to religious cleanliness reasons, their menfolk had to let them go. Wealthier women were usually attended by their serving maids, who would carry the items needed for the ritual bathing, hair removal, and hennaing, which included a large bowl filled with towels, premixed henna, sugar mix or caustic lime for depilation, combs, food, drink, and the high wooden shoes called *pattens* that the ladies wore in the baths to avoid the puddles and other debris. Many of these items would have been given to the women by their husbands as part of their wedding gifts; the richer the men, the more beautiful and highly crafted the combs, shoes, or towels would be. The women often hennaed their hair while in the warm, steamy atmosphere of the hammam, relaxing on mattresses and pillows while the dye worked its magic.

One of the main reasons for visiting the hammam was the postmenstrual cleansing ceremony known as *ghusl,* which was to purify the body and spirit after the passing of blood. To assist in the purification process, the woman would remove all body hair including that of the pubic region, and there are old illustrations depicting women sugaring or applying henna to each other's vulvas, something which often led to discreet attachments between the ladies, as homoerotic activity was not uncommon in the hammam. Depilation, as prescribed by the Prophet Muhammad, involved using a sugar mix or a caustic paste, and henna was then applied to soothe and cool the skin, especially around the tender genital area. This process often left the skin with an altered pH balance and made it very receptive to staining.

The hammam was considered to be a dangerous place to be unprotected, as djinn were attracted to water and, of course, women of reproductive age. Often the resident bath attendant would shout or clap to disperse any djinn that might be lurking in the steam; it was often believed that the djinn would enjoy the hammam at night when the other guests had departed. The use of henna was a formidable repellent for any malevolent djinn, whereas it would attract the kindly spirits, for they were partial to the beauty of the fragrant atmosphere and the beauty of the henna. The patterns applied to their bodies changed from region to region, but the premise was the same: purification and protection from infiltration by bad djinn, and the exhibition of the womens' state of purity and strength.

Ritual Ablutions

The staining of the nails was also used in Muslim cultures from around the fifth century AD. The Prophet Muhammad was said to have encouraged the use of henna on nails, saying that if one is a woman, one must "make a difference to your nails."

Muslim women are discouraged from using nail polish or anything that does not allow water to reach the nail bed, as it interferes with their use of ritual washing, known as *wudu*, which is an important part of their daily worship. So instead they often use henna, as it does not create a barrier for correct purification. This is also something that applies to Orthodox Jewish women, who also observe strict cleansing rituals.

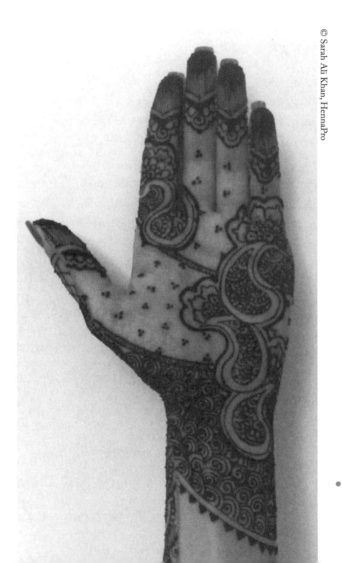

Fingers stained with henna

Chapter 4

Charms, Talismans & Symbols

Khamsa fi ainek ("Five [fingers] in your eye").
—An Arabic saying to ward off the evil eye

· ·

Blessed Henna

Traditionally, henna was used as a form of sympathetic magic, whereby the appropriate symbol painted onto the skin would imbue the wearer with magical power.

In Morocco, the designs used are said to contain *baraka*. Baraka is an Arabic term meaning a blessing or flow of divine grace from God, giving the recipient good fortune or a reward for good deeds performed. If a person is said to "have baraka," he is deemed to be a lucky person or protected by God. Barack Obama's name is a Swahili derivative of the original Arabic. Baraka as a concept is deeply ingrained not only in designs on jewelry, textiles, or other manmade items, but it is said to reside in incenses and plants such as henna. The power is transferred to the object or user through artistry and symbolism. Moroccan henna designs tend to incorporate geometric shapes, eyes, hands, plants, and flowers. Similarly, in India, the symbols are used to placate the gods; the goddess Lakshmi, in particular, is said to dwell in henna designs.

Protection:
The Curse of the Evil Eye

One of the most common uses of symbols or amulets is that of protection. In practically every culture in the world, designs, motifs, and talismans have been created to protect us from evil. Whether that evil comes from a person, an animal, or a spirit, the premise is the same: to create a shield to absorb or bounce back the negative intent. Protective talismans collectively have a name—*apotropaic* (derived from the Greek *apotrepein*, "to ward off").

In many countries, the term *evil eye* differs from how we might perceive it. The person giving the "eye" is not necessarily evil but is harboring jealousy or coveting something or someone; often they will look upon the item or person with envy while praising them. This is believed to cause misfortune for the "overlooked" one and should be prevented or cured by the use of amulets, symbols, spells, and prayers. The evil eye is blamed for anything from ill health, lost love, or the inability to bear children to the death of the household goat or fruit tree.

Examples of the use of talismans, charms, and spells for protection exist throughout the world; in Greece, secret prayers are said that are passed down through the generations for this specific purpose. Once the prayer has been recited, if the person has been afflicted by the evil eye, all present will begin to yawn; this is confirmed and followed by making the sign of the cross and spitting in the air three times. In Turkey and the Middle East, a *nazar* is frequently seen hanging on houses and boats and worn as jewelry. This disk or ball made of glass or stone consists of blue and white concentric circles that represent an eye, and it is believed to reflect evil intent back to the sender. Modernly, the nazar can be seen adorning anything from the tail of an airplane in the Turkish fleet to hanging on mobile phones or baby buggies! (See colour pages for examples of nazars.)

In Islamic and Jewish communities, a prominent protective amulet or design is the hamsa hand (also known as the khamsa or hamesh). It is a depiction of a hand; the word *hamsa* means "five" and therefore is represented by the fingers and thumb and is more commonly known as the Hand of Fatima in the Muslim faith and the Hand of Miriam by Jews. Often a blue eye will be placed in the middle of the hand to deflect evil. The Jewish culture also considers that fish are immune to the influence of the evil eye, and so the symbol is also frequently depicted on the hamsa.

The people of ancient Rome had a slightly more risqué charm to chase away evil intentions: a phallic image called a *fascinum* (derived from the Latin *fascinare*) was used literally to fascinate and divert the evil eye. The *cornicello*, *cornetti*, or "little horn" is a symbol that was often seen worn as a pendant by males, usually made from gold, silver, or red coral. It is an elongated, gently twisted horn shape (often mistaken for a sperm) reputed to represent a sexual organ that would distract the sorcerer from casting their spell. There was also the belief that the evil eye could dry up liquids, and so the male sexual member could seek refuge in the moistness of the female vagina. This may have led to the hand gesture of the clenched fist with the thumb protruding between the index and middle finger, representing the penis within the vagina. This gesture was not only used by the Roman people but was incorporated

*A hamsa hand design
to ward off the evil eye*

into sculpture and made into amulets engraved with magical symbols. Modernly, these charms are still carried by people in countries such as Latin America, where it is viewed as a symbol of good fortune.

Young children have often been seen as being very vulnerable to the evil eye, and in many countries they are protected with amulets, symbols, and/or henna. In Mexico, Latin America, and in Jewish faiths, they are given a bracelet with a bead painted like an eye to repel envy or malice. Because children are believed to be pure and innocent at birth, it is very important that they are protected immediately, and in some cultures newborns are dabbed on the face with kohl, *kumkum* (turmeric or saffron), or henna to make the evil forces believe they are "impure." Young, beautiful girls are often marked behind the ear with henna or kohl to avert the envious or covetous looks of lecherous men or malicious spirits.

Where to Place Your Henna Design

This can depend entirely on what you want to achieve; there are specific places for placing symbols of power (see chapter 8, Henna Spells), but this may not be practical for everyone. Henna also varies in its capacity to stain and the length of time the stain will last, depending on the area of skin it is applied to. Warmer or more porous areas tend to produce the deepest, longest-lasting stain, so the palms of the hands or the soles of the feet tend to soak up the dye, often giving a very deep reddish-black stain, whereas the skin on the upper arm does not seem to produce such a rich colour.

Hands and Fingers

Hands have always been used in many ways throughout different cultures, and we have an almost universal understanding of the majority of the gestures. We understand that offering a hand is a sign of friendship, of a pardon, or to make something binding or legal; the laying of hands on another is a gesture of blessing or healing. Some hand gestures are protective—an outward-facing palm says stop or is used as a shield to bounce back negative energies; a fist can be both threatening and protective. The fingers offer more variations; two fingers in a V are a sign of victory—or, reversed, they become a rude gesture—and a raised middle finger has long been an offensive sign! So where you place your design can mean myriad things.

The palm of the hand is excellent for protective motifs, as the symbol acts as an emblem on your "shield." The palm is warm and will create a deep, dark stain but is also unobtrusive should you not wish to have a symbol fully on display. The stain should last a week to ten days, depending on whether you expose your hands to water a great deal or not. It is probably best to wear protective gloves when washing up or cleaning, as this may cause your design to fade quicker than you would like. Many protective designs are placed on the palm, particularly the talismans against the evil eye that were traditionally used in Morocco. Use bold, strong symbols such as the sun, moon, stars, Eye of Horus, or magical sigils.

• • • • • • • • •

An Eye of Horus

The back of the hands is suitable for more decorative symbolic work, as they will be on display at all times; again, the stain should be quite deep but will wear off quicker the more the hands are immersed in water or detergent. The designs here can be much more intricate and sinuously weave up the arm; a perfect example would be a serpent, commonly used for rising consciousness or divine wisdom.

Fingertips and fingernails are other areas that stain beautifully, but be aware that hennaed nails stay hennaed for several months—they are made from the same protein as hair and are therefore very porous. However, designs on these areas can look stunning and are perfect for protective spells whereby the energy is flowing from the fingertips and deflecting the negative energies away from you. If you don't want to henna the whole nail, you could stencil a small symbol onto one or more nails.

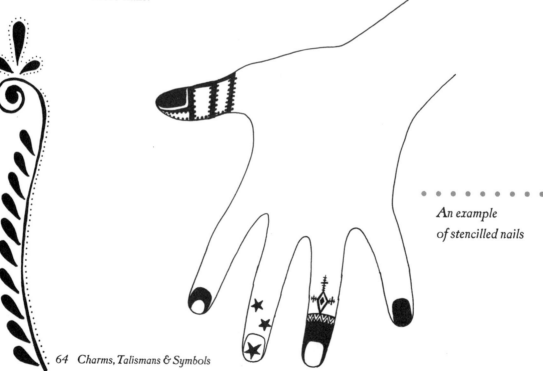

*An example
of stencilled nails*

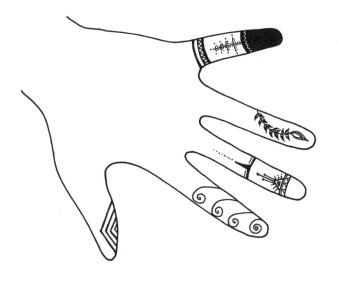

Delicate traceries around the fingers offer a simple yet potent area for applying henna symbols—circles or rings offer protection and/or convey divine or harmonious consciousness.

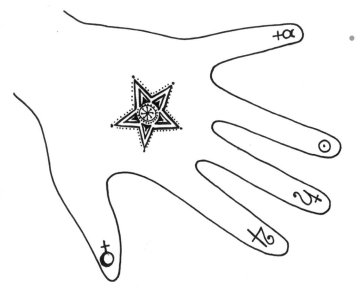

In astrology, the fingers relate to five planets:
- Thumb—Venus
- Index finger—Jupiter
- Middle finger—Saturn
- Ring finger—Sun (also known as the "heart" finger, as people used to believe that it was connected by a nerve or vein to the heart, hence the use of the left finger being used traditionally for the wedding ring)
- Little finger—Mercury

Wrist and Lower Arm

These areas do not stain quite as dark as the hand but still offer a suitable site for weaving traceries, "bracelets," or "arrow"-style designs. Circles, bands, vines, and Moroccan-style Berber patterns all look beautiful on the arm or wrist and can be used for protection, spiritual direction, or general health spells.

Upper Arm and Shoulder

A perfect spot for delicate or very bold "armband" designs. The stain may not be as dark as the hand, but it is a great area for making a statement. On the upper arm, use spirals, vines, or a Celtic band; for the shoulder, go for symbols of strength and vitality like a flaming sun or a phoenix.

Back and Shoulders

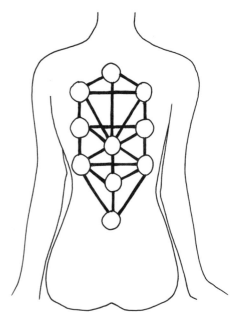

With such a large area, you have the perfect canvas for applying a work of art; obviously, you would need a henna "buddy" to help you with this, as it is impossible to henna your own back! One of the most powerful designs you could use on the back would be the Tree of Life. This ancient symbol can be traced along the spine and contours of the back using an intricate, almost floral design replete with leaves and fruits, or you could use the more geometric Kabbalistic version depicting the ten Spheres, or Sephirot. This design would be used for deep spiritual work or for helping to achieve enlightenment via the branches of wisdom.

*Tree of Life
on the back*

Legs and Ankles

Depending on your skin type, the intensity of the stain can vary; it is easier to shave your legs before applying the henna so that the area is smooth. As legs represent solidity and strength, use this area for courage, growth, and grounding spells—spiral designs, columns, or strings of symbols (such as stars, hieroglyphs, or calligraphy) are good.

Ankles can be used in a similar way to the wrists—circles, bands, and spiraling flowers or vines are perfect designs to symbolize strength and growth.

Soles of the Feet

The soles of the feet symbolize the point whereby we connect with the earth, and this area can be used for any spell that needs a grounding or solid result but can also be used for strong protection against negative influences that may be picked up from our surroundings as we walk. It also represents our will; in antiquity, stepping with the left foot first over a threshold was seen as bad luck, whereas using the right foot would bring good fortune.

Use strong, bold designs, maybe even simply covering the entire skin with henna like the sole of a shoe, for the sole of the foot is often neglected. Not only will the henna nourish the skin, but it will also make you feel as if the wash of deep colour is somehow rooting you to the ground.

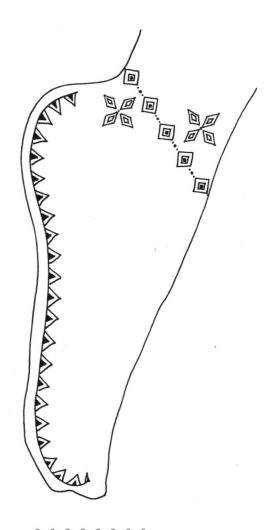

*Example of ankle
and foot designs*

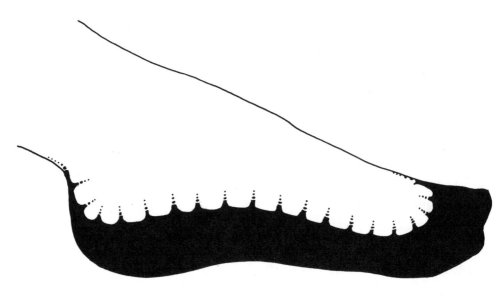

Henna is also very good for cooling the feet and was originally used to protect the feet from the scorching heat of the sun-baked ground or for cooling the body if suffering from heat exhaustion.

The henna will stain the soles very darkly (apart from the arch, which will be slightly lighter) and so will last longer than more exposed areas.

Top of the Foot

This area is wonderful to decorate; you can choose a lacy and intricate pattern like the Indian brides, a strong geometric design of the Berbers, or even a "henna shoe" like *babouches* (Moroccan slippers)! Use this area of the body as a celebration of your path in life—wherever you walk is your destiny. There is a saying that you should "walk your path so that flowers grow in your footsteps"—meaning that everything you do in life should create something beautiful. Designs for the top of the foot can be lighthearted vines, flowers, or stars. Equally, the design can be a reminder to watch where you walk, so be sure to include a protective or strengthening motif as well.

Neck and Décolletage

The skin on these areas does not always produce a very dark stain and tends to exfoliate quite quickly, but it is a beautiful area to add delicate designs to complement the curves or arcs of the neck and collarbone. It may be difficult to henna oneself here, but it is a good canvas for some vines, spirals, or other motifs that signify growth or spirituality.

Breasts

The breast or heart region is the perfect area for love or passion spells—you could even get your lover to henna a personal design to show how much they adore you, or vice versa! The motifs you choose can be lighthearted or very meaningful and should be applied with much love and due caution. The name of your beloved in any chosen script or language is a potent design, as are any symbols including hearts, triangles, shells, flowers, sigils, or circles.

Solar Plexus

The solar plexus is the region between the bottom of the sternum and the belly button, and it is a great area to apply healing, health-promoting designs or ones for psychic awareness. Associated symbols would be the sun, spirals, labyrinths, or other circular shapes. For inward power, a clockwise spiral would be appropriate, whereas for projecting energy outwards, use one that turns anticlockwise.

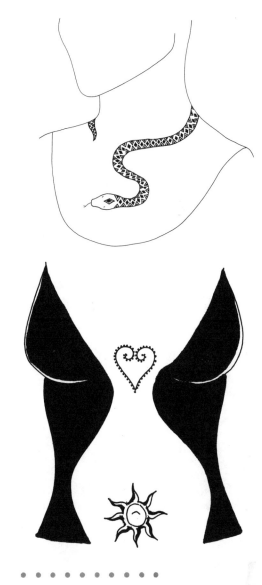

Examples of a snake neck design, top, and heart and solar plexus designs, bottom

Belly

You may find applying henna to the belly to be quite difficult, as you cannot bend or twist without messing up the design; this is where a henna buddy comes in useful, and you need to be prepared to recline for some time while the henna dries. However, designs on the belly or around the navel are very potent, and even if you only manage a small one, it will be not only beautiful to look at but a very powerful talisman.

This area corresponds to the sacral chakra and is an important area for self-esteem and self-respect. It can also be used for healing the organs connected with the abdominal area such as the bowels, ovaries, womb, bladder, and kidneys. Use sensual or bold designs, depending on your intent—weave flowers or vines around the contours of your belly or belly button for soothing or connecting with your feminine energies, or strong, bold designs such as a flaming sun to symbolize self-worth and liberation. If you are pregnant, celebrate the last months with a burst of pattern on your bump.

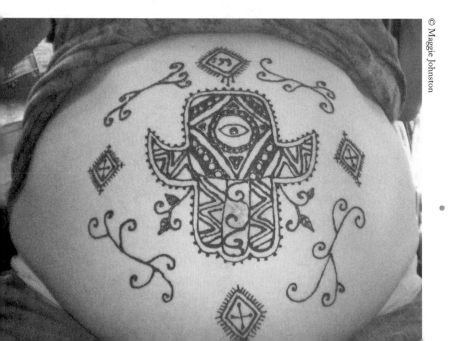

© Maggie Johnston

The Hand of Fatima is a potent symbol to protect against the evil eye, and it imbues good luck and blessings on the wearer

Common Symbols:
Their Meanings and Uses

Use these symbols and their meanings to inspire you to create your magical henna designs. For inspiration, look at designs in other henna, history, or pattern books, clip art libraries, or online.

Acorn: A symbol of good fortune, power, youthfulness and prosperity. A seed of the mighty oak, use this symbol for all small projects that you wish to grow.

Almond: A shape often used in decorative art. As a soft nut within a hard shell, almond represents the essential spirit hidden within.

Alpha (α): The first letter of the Greek alphabet, meaning "beginning." Alpha symbolizes the primeval creation.

Alpha and Omega (α and Ω): The first and last letters of the Greek alphabet, the "beginning" and the "end" respectively, which represent totality and the completeness of God.

Anchor: Hope, consistency, and fidelity.

Angels: Protective and divine presence.

Ankh: The ankh is an ancient Egyptian symbol of a looped cross, symbolizing life and fertility. One of the oldest and most popular symbols used by the Egyptians, it was often depicted in the hands of gods, goddesses, and pharaohs, showing the key to immortality and the power of the Divine. The ankh promotes longevity, the immortality of the soul, and fertility, and offers a link to divine powers.

Ant: Fertility and diligence.

*Clockwise from top left:
ankh, butterfly, caduceus*

Apple: A symbol of fertility, love, and eternity. In the Celtic tradition, it represents spiritual knowledge, due to the inner image of the five-pointed star of the seeds when cut horizontally.

Arrow: A symbol of power and protection, the arrow also symbolizes the rays of the sun and light. It can deflect negative forces when depicted as an outward-projected symbol. In Buddhism and Hinduism, the arrow represents the syllable OM coming from man, who symbolizes a bow—therefore, the arrow journeys from ignorance (the ego) to merge with enlightenment (the Divine).

Axe: A symbol of destruction, therefore useful for protection when something needs a powerful "clearing" action.

Bamboo: Used for good luck or as a symbol of the steps of enlightenment attributed to the knots and sections of the plant.

Bat: A symbol of good luck, intelligence, or sexuality; as a cave dweller, it sometimes symbolizes immortality. Due to its dual nature of being half bird/half mammal, alchemically it represents the hermaphrodite, or duality of the soul.

Beans: Fertility, abundance, and good fortune.

Bear: A masculine (yang) symbol of power and strength; also, alchemically represents the darkness and the prima materia (primal matter, or source of all).

Bee: Used by the ancient Egyptians as a symbol associated with the sun and the human soul, the bee is also a symbol of rebirth, resurrection, diligence, and cleansing.

Bell: The symbol of a bell has been used for centuries to ward off the evil eye and banish malicious spirits. It also represents cosmic harmony. In Islamic traditions, the bell is looked upon as an echo of the voice of God, indicating his omnipotence and allowing the soul to rise above the mundane material world.

Birds: Birds symbolize the link between heaven and earth and are viewed as mediators and embodiments of the soul (as in the Egyptian religion, whereby the *ba*, or soul, is represented by a human-headed bird). Different types of birds have slightly differing meanings, but almost all birds are considered divine mediators.

Butterfly: A symbol of femininity. Two butterflies signify a happy marriage. The butterfly is also universally recognized as a symbol of liberation, metamorphosis, rebirth, and new beginnings.

Caduceus: A herald's staff or wand of the Greek god Hermes (Roman Mercury). It depicts two serpents entwined around the staff, their heads facing each other, and sometimes the serpents are winged. Not to be confused with the wand of Asclepius, the Greek god of healing and medicine, the caduceus is sometimes interpreted as a symbol of fertility, but more often than not it represents balance and equality. In alchemy, it symbolizes the union of opposing forces.

Carp: Strength and stamina. In Japan and China, the carp represents longevity and good fortune, and it is often depicted being ridden by the immortals.

Cat: The symbol of the cat varies; in early years, it was seen as unfortunate except in ancient Egypt, where it was revered. Modernly, it is seen as a symbol of good fortune, wisdom, and protection.

Chai: A Jewish symbol consisting of the Hebrew letters Het (ח) and Yod (י); when written as Chai (חי), they mean "living" or "life."

Chain: Symbolizes attachment or connectivity; often a symbol of the connection between heaven and earth and the uninterrupted flow of energy from the Divine to humankind.

Chalice: See *Cup.*

Child: Innocence and simplicity; a symbol of new beginnings and boundless possibilities.

Chrysanthemum: In Asian countries, it is a symbol of longevity and happiness; also associated with the sun due to its "rays" of petals.

Circle: A symbol of eternity and unity, as it always leads back to itself; it also represents absolute perfection, symmetry, and a reflection of the micro/macrocosms. Use for protection, enlightenment, and spiritual harmony rituals.

THREE INTERSECTING CIRCLES: Symbolizes the trinity of many spiritual paths. Use this design to help connect with any trinity of deities—e.g., Amun, Mut, and Khonsu; Isis, Osiris, and Horus; or the Father, Son, and Holy Spirit.

CIRCLE WITHIN A SQUARE: In the Kabbalah, this represents the spark of the Divine hidden within matter. Use this symbol to connect with your higher self and the Divine.

CIRCLE WITH DOT IN MIDDLE: A symbol of the sun and also of the perfection of humankind. This symbol is useful for all purification, protection, and spiritual progression rituals.

Clockwise from top left:
chalice, cross, dragon,
flower of life (concentric circles)

CONCENTRIC CIRCLES: Also known as the seed of life and the flower of life, many intersecting circles are sacred geometry and represent the spiritual creation and the evolution of humankind.

Clouds: A symbol of spiritual transformation in China, clouds also represent the unseen realm of the gods. Use for enlightenment or communication with the Divine.

Clover: An ancient Celtic magical symbol of vitality and growth, and a symbol of the Trinity in the Middle Ages. Generally thought of as a symbol of good fortune, especially the four- and five-leaf clover. Going clockwise from the left side of the stem, the four leaves represent fame, wealth, love, and health; use for luck, wealth, and good fortune.

Cockerel: A masculine symbol associated with virility, fire, and the sun—also of vigilance, protection, and the power of light over darkness. As a bird, it is also a messenger of the gods.

Column: A symbol of strength representing the connection between earth and the sky (heaven). Can also represent the human body and is linked to the concept of the Tree of Life. Incorporate this design for gaining strength and wisdom and a feeling of connectedness with your community and the spiritual realms.

Cone (also see Triangle): A symbol of spiritual development, leading from the mundane/base to the peak of enlightenment. Also linked to fertility due to its association with the goddesses Astarte, Ishtar, and Aphrodite.

Corn: Prosperity and happiness. Associated in some cultures with the sun and the creation of man.

Crescent (also see Moon): The half moon in its widely used symbolic form—derived from the Latin *crescere,* meaning "to grow"—is attributed to the waxing, or increasing, moon. The waxing moon is indicated by the "horns" of the crescent facing left, and the waning (decreasing) moon is depicted with the horns facing right. One of the most ancient symbols known to humankind, the crescent represents the feminine and is associated with many goddesses of varying cultures. The crescent is often paired with a star or as a pair of crescents flanking a full moon, which symbolizes the Triple Goddess of the Pagans. It represents the moon in astrology and the metal silver in alchemy.

Cross: Another ancient symbol that has many variants. It symbolizes the number four (the four cardinal directions or four quarters) and is used in geometry the world over—the Greek cross is the floor plan of many Byzantine churches, whereas the Latin cross is emulated in churches and cathedrals across the globe and is most well-known as a symbol of the cross of Christ. It represents a "crossroads" either literally or spiritually, symbolizes the intersection of heaven and earth, or indicates the dynamic of masculine (vertical) and feminine (horizontal). It also symbolizes the equinoxes and solstices. The cross placed within a circle represents the perfect human.

Cube (see also Square): Represents the element of earth, solidity, and firmness. Use for grounding and healing.

Cup/Chalice: A symbol of abundance, also a vessel for receiving divine blessings and immortality of the soul. Use for deeply spiritual work or for accepting the grace of (your individual) god.

Diamond: Purity and spirituality. In Morocco, the diamond is a powerful symbol against the evil eye. Use for all protection rituals and to deflect negative or malicious intent.

Disk (see also Circle): A symbol associated with the sun; with wings, it represents the path of the sun through the heavenly realms.

Dolphin: Associated with water/the sea; the dolphin is a spiritual guide and protector.

Dove: Temperance, purity, and the Holy Spirit. The dove is sacred to Ishtar, Aphrodite, and other goddesses of love and fertility; it is also a symbol of peace through reconciliation.

Dragon: An ambiguous symbol, the dragon can represent many things in different cultures. In China and Japan, the dragon is believed to bestow good fortune and fertility, and it is a protector against demons. In Hinduism and Taoism, it can produce the elixir of life and represents immortality. However, in other cultures, it is a symbol of evil or the battle between our ego and our regressive forces. It also symbolizes a duality of the masculine, active yang energy but with the watery forces of yin—an alchemical, primeval blend of opposites. A powerful symbol, use dragon for good luck, protection, fertility, balance, or strength.

Dragonfly: These delightfully colourful and somewhat mystical creatures are a symbol of transformation and cutting through the binds of illusion. They also represent joyful freedom, beauty, and direction. Use for any work where you feel trapped by false illusion and wish to "fly free" and be transformed.

Duck (also see Bird): In China, a pair of ducks symbolizes marital stability and bliss. Use for harmony and marriage rituals.

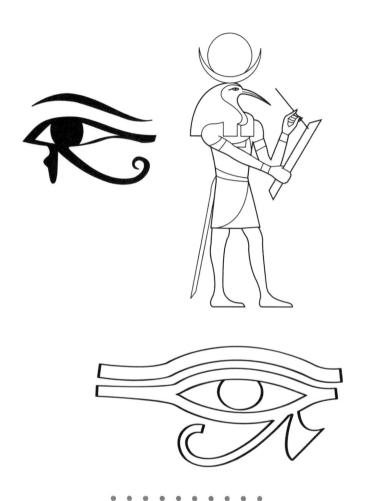

Clockwise from top left:
left Eye of Horus, Thoth, and
right Eye of Horus

Egg: In universal creation myths, the egg represents a primary part of the primeval birth of the world. The egg floated in the waters that were created from chaos and issued forth the cosmos and the elements; various deities were depicted being born from the egg. Therefore, it is seen as a symbol of perfection, birth/rebirth, or the alchemical prima materia from which the philosopher's stone was hatched. Use for fertility, rebirth, or "connecting to the source" rituals.

Eye: Associated with the sun, light, spirit, inner vision, and protection. Use for all magic where you desire wisdom, prosperity, spiritual protection, good health, or clairvoyant powers.

The Eye of Horus—or *udjat*, the ancient Egyptian "all-seeing eye"—was traditionally believed to give the deceased the power to see again. The right eye represented the sun and protection (Re), and the left eye, the moon and magic (Thoth). It was also a system of sacred geometry and mathematics.

The evil eye is a very prominent concept in the Middle East, whereby the casting of a look or glance from someone (or something) who means you harm or is jealous of you can be very damaging. This is basically the premise for sympathetic "black" magic—of being cursed or hexed—and is a worldwide belief. There are many different amulets or symbols used to protect oneself from the evil eye, one of which is the predominantly Turkish nazar, a ball or disk usually made from glass with concentric rings of blue and white circles that represent the eye and therefore protect against any negative influences by bouncing the evil back to the person who cast it. These amulets are often seen in Mediterranean, Islamic, and Middle Eastern countries.

The Eye of Providence, or "all-seeing eye"—an eye set within a triangle and often surrounded with rays of light, or glory—is a symbol of the

omnipresence of the Divine. Closely aligned with the Egyptian udjat, it is now universally linked to Freemasonry and the ideal of a Supreme Being watching over humankind and making the Mason aware that every thought and deed is observed, which helps them strive to be moral men.

Faeries: Symbols of the spirit of nature that must be treated with caution. Use the image of a faerie to draw good fortune towards you and to show your respect for the earth.

Feather: Often associated with the sun, the sky, and material or spiritual growth. The feather of Ma'at is the symbol of truth, order, and justice, as worn by the Egyptian goddess of the same name, who presided over the weighing of the heart in the Hall of Judgment.

Fig/Fig Leaf: Symbolizes fertility, abundance, knowledge, and nourishment. Use for any magic that requires joyous bounty.

Fire/Flame: Represents purification and spiritual rebirth (see Phoenix). Use fire or flames in a design when you wish to renew, purify, strengthen, or protect yourself.

Fish: Closely associated with water, its life source, the fish is symbolic of life, rebirth, and fertility. Symbolic of the astrological sign of Pisces, the fishes represent the passive, feminine, and moveable.

Fleur-de-lys: A symbol of the Trinity, of purity, and of martial power.

Flower: Associated with the sun, rain, and femininity. The flower, or blossom, represents achievement, the ability to absorb knowledge, and humility. Choose your favourite flower and use it to connect you with the manifestation and beauty of nature.

Frog: Another ambiguous symbol, depending on culture; in China and Japan, the frog augers good luck, whereas in the Bible, frogs were seen as unclean or evil. In Egypt, they represent fertility and immortality. In shamanic traditions, frogs are seen as a symbol for spiritual cleansing. Use for cleansing, good fortune, or fertility motifs.

Grapes/Grapevine: A symbol of abundance, rebirth, and life itself. This design could be easily incorporated on an arm, leg, or back.

Hammer: Symbolizes power, strength, justice, and reasoning. Associated with the Norse god Thor and revered in Celtic traditions, this is a very strong fire symbol to use in spells for legal or authoritarian matters or direction of will.

Hand: The hand is used symbolically and practically in many different ways—to make gestures that are protective, offensive, or victorious; as a handshake to offer friendship, make something binding, or to indicate openness. Symbolic or magical hand gestures are used in traditional dance in Indian cultures and in Buddhist traditions for meditation. The left hand is commonly seen as feminine and passive, whereas the right is masculine and conveys activity or blessing. The use of the hand as a design symbol indicates power, divine blessing (the hand of God), or, in the form of the hamsa (the Hand of Fatima or Miriam—see page 61), as a powerful protective motif.

Hare: A powerful fertility symbol associated with spring, the earth, and renewal. Also symbolizes fleetness, agility, and sexuality.

Heart: Generally regarded as a symbol of love but also associated with the will, spirituality, and the centre of reasoning. In ancient Egypt, the heart was viewed as the central point for the life force, the will, and the mind. In Islam, it is identified with contemplation and spiritual love, and in India,

Clockwise from top left: fish,
fleur-de-lys, Hecate's wheel, horse,
Eastern lotus, Egyptian lotus

it is perceived as the place of contact between humans and God (Brahma). Use for all love spells but also for a deep connection to the Divine.

Hecate's Wheel: A labyrinth-like symbol associated with the Greek goddess Hecate. It represents her triple aspect of Maiden, Mother, and Crone, and possibly is linked to Hecate's early role as guardian of crossroads, before her gradual change to goddess of magic. Use this symbol as a connection to your female roles and for any spell that involves taking a firm direction towards a goal.

Hieroglyphs: Derived from the Greek to mean "sacred writing" and used as stylized pictures by the ancient Egyptians to form their alphabet.

Horn: Power and fertility. It is an ambivalent symbol that is feminine in its lunar aspect (shaped like a crescent) or masculine in its phallic shape. Also represents abundance when depicted as a horn of plenty. Use as a motif to create balance between the masculine and feminine aspects of the self or for a powerful protective symbol.

Horse: Fertility, power, energy, and freedom. Associated with Celtic goddesses Epona and Rhiannon but equally seen as a masculine symbol of virility and strength. Use as a balance of male/female energies and for strength and stamina.

Horseshoe: A universal symbol of good luck, often used in Egypt with "horse beads" to ward off the evil eye. Incorporate in designs to add extra protection against negative energies.

Hourglass: A symbol of the fleeting passage of time. Useful incorporated into designs as a reminder to make the most of our time on earth.

Ibis: A bird sacred to Thoth, the Egyptian god of magic and writing. Its curved beak represents the lunar energies. Use in spells to invoke the wisdom of Thoth in all his aspects.

Ivy: As an evergreen, it is a symbol of immortality but also one of fidelity and friendship. In ancient Greece, it was customary to present the bride and groom with a bunch of ivy. Use in all spells involving friendship, fidelity, or eternal love.

Jackal: Represents Anubis, the ancient Egyptian god of embalming and the afterlife. He assisted with the weighing of the heart in the Hall of Judgment and was the guardian of the underworld. Use for any work involving astral projection or travelling through the spirit world. Jackal is also a powerful protection design to apply if you are to undergo a general anesthetic.

Key: A symbol of liberation and freedom, also for success and unlocking hidden knowledge and wisdom. Use for any work involving new or unknown situations or for gaining access to secrets or hidden wisdom.

Knife: A symbol of masculine, active energy; also for cutting through negative vices or thoughts. Use for banishing rituals or for evoking strong masculine energy.

Knot: Symbolizes connectivity or a link to greater powers for protection or to bestow immortality. In ancient Egypt, the "Knot of Isis" was a common amulet, similar to the ankh, worn to encourage a long life. It is also connected to love and marriage; in some cultures, the hands are knotted together either symbolically or literally. It is used as a protective symbol in Islam; the men often tie knots in their beards to ward off evil. The action of untying or cutting through a knot is also symbolic of opening oneself up or overcoming problems. Use for any work that involves protection, ridding bad habits, or strengthening bonds.

Labyrinth: Associated with initiation rites, use this symbol as a personal quest to enter the spiritual realms and traverse the light and dark worlds or for meditation to reach the "hidden" centre, or God.

Ladder: As a representation of the steps between heaven and earth, incorporate this design to help achieve spiritual progress.

Leaf: A much-used design in henna patterns, the leaf represents happiness and prosperity. When depicted as a branch with leaves, it's a symbol of community and cooperation.

Letters: Highly symbolic in many cultures, especially within the Jewish Kabbalah. Each letter can be mystically interpreted by its shape, numerical value, and pronunciation. In ancient Greece, much emphasis was put on the seven vowels and their symbolic link with the seven heavenly spheres and the seven sets of stars that moved within them. The vowels were perceived as symbols of spirit whereby the consonants were symbolic of matter; put together within the alphabet, both spirit and matter were blended to create perfection and completeness. In the Muslim world, letters are categorized as being of the four elements—earthy, airy, fiery, or watery.

Write your name or initials in calligraphy or calligraphic style for added power.

Lightning: In its positive form, lightning represents a manifestation of divine, or "greater," power, fertility, or even phallic energy. In its other form,

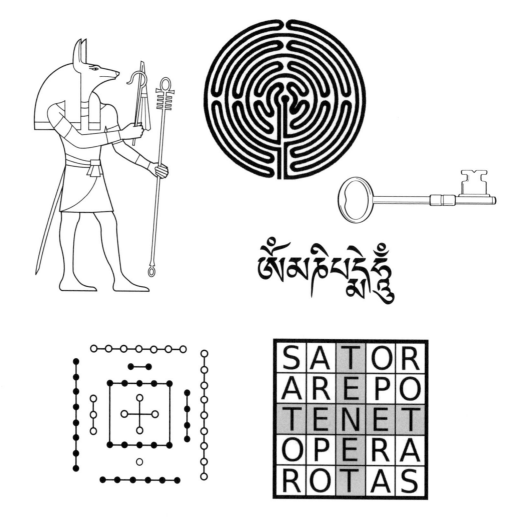

Clockwise from top left: Anubis, labyrinth, key, Om mani padme hum, "Sator" magic square, magic square with dots

lightning is a symbol of divine wrath or punishment. Use for potent magic needing divine energy and direction.

Lion: A symbol of strength and power, associated with the sun, the astrological sign of Leo, and the Egyptian goddess Sekhmet. Use this symbol for all work that involves the need for courage, strength, and justice.

Lizard: A light-seeker and therefore symbolic of those who seek spiritual enlightenment; associated with the sun. The lizard is a lovely design to use for any work where you need guidance towards the light of divinity.

Lotus: One of the most ancient and beautiful symbols. The lotus has played a vital role in the spiritual symbolism of ancient Egypt, India, and East Asia. As a flower that follows the natural patterns of the day and night, it was viewed as one of the most sacred plants. In the morning, the tightly closed bud opens only when the sun has risen, and then when the sun sets, it draws itself back under the water to await the light once more. However, not only is it revered for its affinity with the light and dark but also its remarkable ability to live within the mud and detritus of the river, only to emerge each day pure and unsullied. The ancient Egyptians' relationship with the lotus is evident from its depiction on tombs, temples, and papyri; the flower is featured in several of their creation myths, whereby it emerges from the primeval waters of chaos and opens to reveal the divine one. Its ability to emerge each day with the sun linked it to the sacred, life-giving aspect of the Nile, and it became a symbol of immortality and regeneration. The blue lotus of the Nile (*Nymphaea caerulea*) is believed to be a narcotic and was probably used in rituals to evoke a trancelike state for meditation or astral projection.

The lotus is also found in the Buddhist and Hindu traditions. Again, it is featured in creation myths and revered for its purity. The eight-petaled lotus is a symbol of the cardinal points and so encompasses cosmic harmony, whereas the thousand-petaled lotus symbolizes the entirety of spiritual revelation. Buddha is often depicted sitting on a lotus leaf or emerging from the flower, and the mantra *Om mani padme hum* translates as "Praise to the jewel in the lotus, hail!" whereby the jewel relates to the mind/consciousness and the lotus is the heart, the source of love.

Use the symbol of the lotus for any magical work that involves contemplation or meditation upon the source of creation (the Divine), and also for purification, protection, or opening your heart.

Magic Squares: Used as talismans for divination, protection, and longevity for over 4,000 years. Particularly favored by early Arabic polymaths, they became popular in the middle ages in Europe with the growth of magic and mysticism, and Agrippa's *kameas*—the term used by medieval and Renaissance magicians to refer to the various magic squares in use during that period—are still used in ceremonial magic today. Numbers are used to correspond with planetary or angelic forces. One of the most widely recognized is the Sator Square, which uses the words SATOR AREPO TENET OPERA ROTAS as a palindrome in a square reading the same top to bottom, bottom to top, left to right, and right to left. It is believed to translate from the Latin as "The Great Sower holds in his hand all works; all works the Great Sower holds in his hand."[13]

Mandala: Derived from the Tibetan language, *mandala* is the Sanskrit word for "circle" or "completeness." It relates to the concentric circular

13 C. W. Ceram, *The March of Archeology*, 30.

patterns used in Buddhist and Hindu traditions as a meditational tool. The psychologist Carl Jung referred to mandalas as "a representation of the unconscious self"—they are also a symbol of the micro- and macrocosm.

Mistletoe: An ancient Celtic symbol of immortality and good luck.

Moon (see also Crescent): A strongly passive feminine symbol due to the moon's influence on women's bodies and the oceans. Representative of all things connected with the female psyche and physical body, fertility, the power of change, good luck, and the unconscious realms. Use for spells involving clairvoyance or dreams, fertility, female protection and health, astral projection, or any work in the spirit world.

> TRIPLE MOON: This is a symbol representing the three phases of the moon as waxing, full, and waning, and also the aspects of the Pagan Goddess as Maiden, Mother, and Crone. Associated with female energies and psychic abilities, this is a traditional symbol often worn by high priestesses. This symbol can help to enhance your feminine energy and psychic abilities; use it for divination and ritual magic.

Nefer: A symbol depicting the heart and trachea, it was originally worn by the Egyptians to represent beauty, goodness, health, and youthfulness.

Numbers: As symbols, the numbers can be used literally or as the amount of other images in the design, e.g., six hearts.

> ZERO: All, everything, the absolute.

> ONE: Individuality, yang (positive, masculine), aggressive, new beginnings, and purity.

> TWO: Balance, union, yin (passive, feminine), receptivity, duality, and relationships.

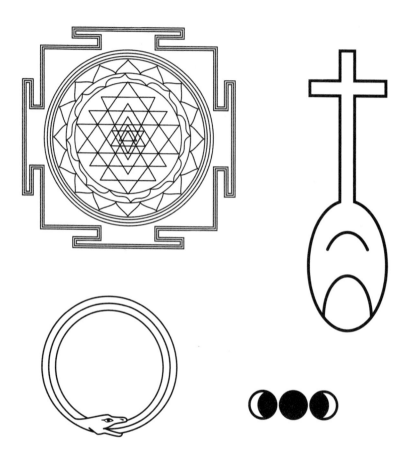

Clockwise from top left:
mandala, nefer, triple moon, ouroboros

THREE: Creativity, fecundity, direction, and new ventures; also past, present, and future.

FOUR: Stability, solidity, grounding, persistence.

FIVE: Motion, travel, unpredictability, change.

SIX: Harmony, love, truth, balance, enlightenment.

SEVEN: Magical influence, activity, consciousness.

EIGHT: Power, money, success, determination, evolution.

NINE: Highest level of achievement, attainment, intellect, and power to change.

Oak Leaf: As a part of the mighty oak tree, the leaf symbolizes strength, masculinity, and tenacity. Use for rituals that need strength, fortitude, and incorruptibility.

Octagon: The eight-sided shape represents universality and perfection. In the ancient Egyptian religion, there were eight spheres to ascend to, which included the seven planets and the eighth sphere of perfection.

OM (also AUM): The sacred syllable used by Hindus, Buddhists, and Jains to represent, in part, the three stages of life or the all-encompassing entity that is God. Used as a meditational tool and at the beginning and ending of prayers or readings from the Vedas, the sacred texts of Hinduism. The sacred Sanskrit scripture, the Katha Upanishad, describes the OM: "The goal, which all Vedas declare, which all austerities aim at, and which humans desire when they live a life of conscience, I will tell you briefly, it is Aum."

Use the symbol (ॐ) to meditate on as a visual reminder of the all-encompassing nature of the Divine and our role within the world from birth to death.

Ouroboros: A very ancient symbol of a serpent eating its own tail, the name *ouroboros* is derived from the Greek word meaning "tail swallower." Its origin is most likely Egypt, where it was used as a sign of the cycle of life, regeneration, and the passage of the sun god on his daily travels between the light and the dark of day and night. In alchemy, the ouroboros represents Mercury and the process of purification, renewal, and immortality. Use in all workings to empower you for the understanding of life and death, and for purification and spiritual regeneration.

Owl: Knowledge and the ability to penetrate the spiritual darkness to understand our higher nature. Sacred to the goddess Athena, the owl also brings good luck. Use in spells where you need to gain spiritual knowledge of those things hidden to you.

Peacock: A symbol with varied meanings but universally known as a solar symbol and one of immortality and beauty. However, the negative symbolism is that of pride and vanity. In India, it is a common motif, where it is often depicted being ridden by various deities. Use for spells involving spiritual beauty and the healing power of the sun.

Pear: The pear is often seen as a sexual symbol, of fertility and fecundity, representative of the female form. Use in spells to create a fertile ground for any physical or personal projects but also to encourage the "fruit of the womb" (baby power)!

Phoenix: Seen as a sacred bird in many traditions, the ancient Egyptians named it the benu bird, and it appeared in several different forms. It was associated with the creator sun god, the daily course of the sun, and the renewal of life, as experienced by the yearly inundation of the Nile that produced new and fertile life. This concept was adopted by the Greeks and

Romans and eventually by the church fathers, who took on the phoenix as a symbol of regeneration, the bird regularly consumed by fire to resurrect itself from the ashes. Use this beautiful bird as a symbol of the triumph of life over death, of spiritual rebirth and immortality of the soul.

Pig: A potent fertility symbol since antiquity due to its amazing capacity to breed, the sow is often associated with earth-mother-type goddesses. Generally perceived as a symbol of happiness, good fortune, and fecundity, although in some cultures it is seen to represent gluttony, lack of chastity, or plain ignorance. Use in spells for fertility, abundance, and to promote good luck.

Pine Cone: Used for millennia as a symbol of fertility.

Plants: All plants are symbolic of growth and constant change; they are representative of the ability to thrive from earthly goodness and as such encompass the four elements. Use a plant design to create unity and to build a relationship with all the good things that our planet can offer for our nourishment and survival—earth, air, fire (sun), and water.

Pomegranate: Like other seed-bearing fruit, the pomegranate is a symbol of fertility and, because of its sensuous flesh, femininity and sexuality. Its redness is associated with blood, and so it also represents the cycle of life and death. Use as a symbol to celebrate feminine beauty and sexual maturity, and also as a potent protection against infertility.

Poppy: Sleep and forgetfulness. Use in a design to help overcome worries and trauma or to assist in powerful dreams.

Quince (see also Apple): In ancient times, the quince was associated with love, happiness, and fertility. It is possible that Aphrodite's "apple" was, in fact, a quince, for it was common for Greek women to bring the fruit into

• • • • • • • • • •

Clockwise from top left:
owl, peacock, phoenix, ram

the home of their husband on their wedding day to guarantee a happy and fertile marriage.

Rainbow: Symbolizes union between the earthly realm and the heavens and the connection between humans and the Divine. Use this symbol for spells that involve spiritual unity and the desire for a better world.

Raindrop: Another fertility symbol due to the ability of rain to encourage growth. Use stylized raindrops in a design for fertility and hope spells, whether for ideas, projects, or babies.

Ram: Attributed to the astrological sign of Aries or Knum, the Egyptian god of creation, the ram is a potent strength and fertility symbol.

Rhombus: Due to its shape being symbolically suggestive of the female genitalia, the rhombus is a sign of feminine sexuality and fertility.

Ribbon: Symbolizes binding or releasing. Use for marriage or handfasting (or, conversely, breaking up or divorce), or for legal- or love-related designs.

Right and Left: The right side is generally seen as masculine, active, and just, whereas the left is passive, feminine, and merciful. However, in some traditions, the left is associated with evil or unluckiness and the right with morality and spirituality, hence the ancient bias against left-handed people.

Ring: Another symbol of eternity due to a ring having no beginning and no end. A symbol of unity, fidelity, or authority similar to the circle or the eye, the ring has properties that protect against negative or malevolent forces. Use for love, marriage, devotion (mental, physical, or spiritual), and protection spells.

River: Symbolic of impermanence and fluidity but also of continual renewal. The merging of rivers into the sea represents the unity of all things. Use

fluid, streaming lines in your design to reflect the passage of time but also the beauty of letting things wash over you. In China, they encourage people to "be like water"—meaning to flow around all that comes in your way.

Rose: The eternal symbol for love, beauty, and purity. In alchemy, the seven-petaled rose was considered a complex symbol of correspondences or the steps of the alchemical process, and the "rose cross" of the Rosicrucians symbolizes the spiritual Great Work. Use in rituals or spells that involve love (human or divine) or purity of heart in regard to spiritual work.

Runes: An ancient script originally used in Germanic and Celtic tribes before the introduction of Latin. Each rune is representative of a letter and was also used for magical and divinatory purposes. However, the use of runes continued until the fifteenth century, where they were prevalent in medieval Norway.

Salamander: A mythical elemental who was believed to be able to live within fire and remain unharmed, salamanders symbolize how the righteous can remain peaceful even when under attack. Use this delightful creature as a powerful protector should you feel attacked for no reason—mentally, physically, or spiritually.

Scales: Symbolizes justice and balance; also the sign for Libra in the zodiac. Use whenever you need a clear and balanced decision or outcome.

Scarab: Also known as the dung beetle, the scarab was revered in ancient Egypt as *khepri,* or "he who has come into being," a symbol of resurrection and solar energy. Egyptians believed the scarab had been created out of a ball of dung, and the action of rolling the dung ball and burying it in the sand to lay their eggs in was deeply symbolic of the daily passage of the sun, the life force of the world. Therefore, the scarab became a deeply symbolic emblem in their religious and daily lives, representing creation, resurrection, and eternal life. Use the design of this endearing but powerful beetle to bring yourself closer to the source of creation, to enhance the routine of your daily spiritual quest, or to symbolize the desire for immortality of the soul.

Scorpion: Aside from being the zodiacal sign of Scorpio, the scorpion was also a highly feared yet revered sacred animal in ancient Egypt. Serqet, the goddess of magic, was depicted as a woman with a scorpion on her head and was both a protective and a punishing deity. Those who she felt were unjust or immoral would be struck by the poison of the scorpion, yet she also gave breath to the justified deceased, allowing them to be reborn in the afterlife. She also protected humans and gods from scorpion stings, snake bites, or other venomous attacks, and she particularly favored and protected pregnant women and children. Use the symbol of the scorpion as a protective design against injustice and maliciousness or to overcome the negative quality of self-destruction.

Sea Horse: An endearing symbol of good luck. In early China, sea horses were perceived as an escort of souls to the afterlife.

Serpent: This creature is probably one of the most revered yet reviled on the planet. Worshipped as a deity amongst some cultures, seen as the personification of evil in others, it certainly has a powerful effect on the human psyche. Its ability to shed its skin and devour other creatures with ease has given the snake an uneasy place in our history that still evokes a response today. Love them or hate them, snakes are a symbol of renewal, hidden power (see Uraeus), and protection. It is also a highly sexual masculine and feminine symbol (for its phallic shape and its copious

Clockwise from top left:
sma, spiral, pentagram,
hexagram, sea horse

receptivity, respectively), and it is used as a metaphor for the powerful energy of tantric kundalini, coiled at the base of the spine, which rises through the spiritual centers until unity with the Divine is achieved. The serpent devouring its own tail is an ancient symbol of renewal and the cycle of life and death (see ouroboros). Use the image of a snake for magic involving sexuality, protection, or rebirth.

Shell: A symbol of perfection, for the shape of certain shells reflects the principle of the golden ratio, or the golden spiral, believed to be the measurement used by God for the creation of all things. The scallop shell is sacred to the biblical James, son of Zebedee, and has been worn for centuries by the pilgrims on the sacred Way of St. James to his shrine at Santiago de Compostela in Spain.[14] It is also reputed to be a potent symbol of fertility. Use the motif of the shell for any work involving sacred contemplation on the creation of all things or for interpreting the direction of your life.

Sickle: A symbol of time, death, and the harvest that renews each year; also associated with the crescent as a lunar symbol.

Skull: The skull, aside from its association with death and impermanence, is symbolic of the human microcosm and our relationship with the universal macrocosm. It is also a symbol of transformation. Use the skull when contemplating the transience of our human existence or when you need a reminder to use your time on this earth with respect and purpose.

14 A major Christian pilgrimage route used for over a thousand years and modernly made famous by the author Paulo Coelho in his book *The Pilgrimage.*

Sma: An ancient Egyptian symbol representing the lungs. When placed on a mummy, it was believed to give breathing power to the deceased.

Snail: A lunar symbol also associated with the spiral and femininity due to its shape, which is seen as a representation of female genitalia. In some American Indian traditions the snail is believed to help protect pregnant women due to its shape and encasing shell.

Snowflake: Individuality and perfection. No two snowflakes are alike, just as no two humans can be completely alike, but it is the individual nature that reflects the perfect beauty of the creation. Snowflakes embody purity and geometric perfection, a reminder of our spiritual goal to become as pure and perfect as divinity. Use this symbol to celebrate your inner individuality and to invoke purification.

Spear or Lance: A strongly masculine and phallic symbol but also one that implies direction, strength, and power. Use in spells where direct action and bravery is needed or to pierce through negative qualities or vices.

Sphere: Symbolic of the universe and the union of opposites, the self, and the relationship between humans and nature. Its use is similar to that of the circle or ring, but it's also symbolic of completeness, perfection, and universal divinity and worship.

Spider (see also **Web***):* Power and growth; femininity; mystery, creation and progress. Also associated with the number eight—the number of infinity.

Spiral: Probably the oldest symbol connected to human spirituality and our relationship with the natural and supernatural world. Historically, the spiral has been found in prehistoric sites around the world and is most likely attributed to the cycles of nature and the phases of the moon and its influence on bodies of water and the human condition. It is often used by modern Pagans as a symbol of the Goddess, and when used ritually it can enhance psychic vision, assist in shamanic or astral wandering, and provide spiritual protection.

Square: The four corners are believed to divert evil influences. A symbol of earth and matter, the square is foundational and static, often seen in relation to the circle, which represents the sky or heaven. It is symbolic of the four elements and four cardinal directions, and when placed next to the circle it is seen as the embodiment of pure beauty. Use in conjunction with elemental magic or in protection spells.

Staff (see also Caduceus): An emblem of magical power, knowledge, and healing used to drive away evil. It can also be a phallic symbol. Use the design for direction of magical energy and for healing work.

Stars: Hope and cosmic unity.

PENTAGRAM: A five-pointed star usually drawn in one movement. Amongst other things, it represents the five elements of air, fire, water, earth, and spirit, and the figure of a human being. Used for centuries by various traditions, the pentagram can symbolize knowledge and health or can protect the user from evil spirits. The star is normally depicted "point up" when used for magical purposes to represent the power of spirit over the elements, whereas the inverted pentagram represents the descent of spirit into matter and is considered negative or, in the case of Satanic use, evil. The pentagram is often seen enclosed in a circle (called a pentacle), which symbolizes the integration of body and spirit. Use this symbol as a powerful protective design or to create balance between the five elements.

Clockwise from top left:
six-, seven-, eight-, and nine-pointed stars

HEXAGRAM: The well-known symbol of a six-pointed star formed from two triangles, also called the Star of Solomon or Star of David. It is a symbol of the joining of opposites, the interpenetration of the invisible and visible worlds, and is composed of the alchemical symbols of the four elements. Use this as a design to assist in elemental magic, alchemy, protection, or any work that involves connecting the material with the spiritual.

THE UNICURSAL HEXAGRAM: The six-pointed star but drawn in one movement as opposed to the two triangles placed one over the other. It is symbolic of supreme self-confidence and the ability to achieve adepthood; in Pagan symbolism, it is representative of the solar system.

HEPTAGRAM: Also known as a septagram, or seven-pointed star. The number seven is sacred in all the major religions and is mentioned in context in all the holy books; not only does it represent the seven planets, seven levels of heaven, seven days of creation, and seven deadly sins, but it is the number of perfection or completeness. In the Wiccan tradition, it is associated with faeries and often referred to as the "elven star." Use the heptagram or any seven-sided shape as a powerful protection symbol.

EIGHT-POINTED STAR: Used in many cultures, the eight-pointed star universally symbolizes harmony, balance, and cosmic order. The eight points reflect the four quarters, solstices, and equinoxes. Use this design to connect with cosmic creation, time, and space.

NINE-POINTED STAR: A symbol of unity or a representation of the nine planets. Used in the Baha'i faith to represent the nine world religions. This design offers good fortune, spiritual strength, and understanding.

Sun: One of the most important symbols known to humankind due to its light and life-giving properties, for without the sun we would not survive. As it rises and sets each day, it has been revered as a symbol of resurrection and renewal; its daily passage across the skies has been sacred to all cultures. It represents the highest cosmic power, and solar deities from around the world are well known for their creational abilities. Usually attributed to the masculine, active principles, the sun is associated with the metal gold and the element of fire. As a design, the sun is especially powerful for people born under the astrological sign of Leo and for those needing healing or spiritual growth, and for bringing general well-being and good fortune. When depicted as a flaming sun, it is particularly powerful as a protective or banishing symbol. Use for "burning away" negative energies or vices.

Sword: Masculinity, strength, courage, and martial power; also connected with the sun. Due to its sharp blade, it is seen as an emblem of decisiveness, justice, and the ability to cut through evil. Use for all work that involves precision, strength, courage, and the ability to sever negative or destructive thoughts or influences.

Tau: The nineteenth letter of the Greek alphabet: Σ. Also the Tau cross, named after the last letter of the Hebrew alphabet but believed to have originated with the Egyptians and later used by the early Christians. It is a symbol of resurrection, reincarnation, and redemption; in Egypt, the pharaoh would have the Tau raised to his lips during initiation into the Mysteries. It represents new beginnings and can be used in initiation ceremonies and any rituals that involve a fresh start, or for accessing hidden mysteries.

Tiger: This awesome animal is a symbol of physical strength, spiritual ability, and immortality. Use in any spells that require great focus and courage.

Tree: An ancient and powerful symbol used in many cultures as a representation of nature or divine beings. Deciduous trees symbolize rebirth and resurrection; an evergreen is symbolic of immortality. The shape of the tree represents the union of the cosmos—the roots in the underworld, its trunk on the material plane, and its crown in the heavens. It can be an ambiguous symbol in that it is protective and feminine, bearing fruit and offering shelter and protection; or, conversely, it could be seen as masculine due to its huge strength and the phallic nature of the trunk. The Tree of Life has many meanings, offering abundance and knowledge or, in Kabbalistic terms, representing the process of Creation, of how God made the world out of nothing, and the ten points (known as Sephirot) are the ten attributes of God through which he shows himself and continues to create on both the physical and spiritual levels. It is effectively a map for us to become as or at one with God by reflecting his actions and attributing them to ourselves and our lives.

Triangle: Symbolizes masculinity when tip points upwards, femininity when tip points downwards. Associated with light, fire, the number three, and the Trinity, the triangle often appears with a hand, an eye, a head, or the Hebrew name of God. A protective sign, it is used magically by most metaphysical traditions including Freemasonry (see Eye of Providence, page 81), Hermetics, and in alchemy as the three stages of development (both spiritual and physical). Use the triangle in conjunction with the eye symbol for a powerfully protective design. The sharp corners also deflect negative influence, and it is a reminder of the Divine's all-seeing and protective nature.

Clockwise from top left:
uraeus, Tau cross, triquetra in a circle,
yin/yang, triskele

Triquetra: From the Latin meaning "triangle." In Paganism, it is a Celtic symbol of the Triple Goddess and the god Odin. Associated with the magical aspect of the number three, it represents the three phases of the Goddess (Maiden, Mother, Crone), whereas in Christianity it symbolizes the Holy Trinity. Use this unique design to attune to the power of three—the Goddess, the trinities of ancient Egypt (Amun, Mut, Khonsu or Isis, Osiris, Horus) or of the Christian faith (Father, Son, Holy Spirit).

Triskele or Triskelion: Meaning "three-legged" in Greek, the triskele is a shape made by three interlocked protrusions such as spirals, legs, or horns. It is believed to be an ancient Neolithic symbol representing the power of life and rebirth. In Wicca, like the triquetras (see above), it symbolizes the phases of the Triple Goddess and other triplicities; in Christianity, it represents the Trinity. The horned triskelion, or Odin's Horn, is used by followers of the Norse Asatru religion. Use the design for connection with the ancient powers of the trinities and for celebrations of life and the promise of rebirth.

Uraeus (see also Serpent): The sacred upright cobra placed on the crown of an Egyptian pharaoh or depicted on a god or goddess as a sign of royalty or divine authority. The cobra was also representative of the goddess Wadjet (who protected the pharaoh), symbolic of the pharaoh's enlightened spiritual state as a Divine One on earth. Use for achieving spiritual progress and enlightenment and for divine protection.

Web: A symbol that embodies our creative or personal progress in life and the far-reaching consequences of our actions. The symbol of the web makes us think about how we should weave our own destiny, to serve us or trap us.

Use this motif whenever you need to contemplate your place in the universe and to give you inspiration and insight into how to apply changes or new directions.

Wishbone: A symbol of good luck and to make wishes and dreams come true.

Yin/Yang: A Chinese symbol representing the two opposing forces in conjunction; also dualities—male and female, dark and light, high and low. Use the symbol to create balance, interconnectedness, and constant interaction, and to highlight the continual link between natural opposites.

Chapter 5

Herbs and Oils
in Henna Magic

Alchemy neither composes nor mixes: it increases and activates
that which already exists in a latent state.
—Franz Hartmann

· ·

Almost Alchemy

Using herbs and oils is a kind of alchemy, for these substances come from the amalgamation of the four elements—earth, air, fire, and water. Every plant and tree needs these four things to be able to grow from a tiny seed into a beautiful creation, and it is from this we can gather the fruits of that process in the form of leaves, bark, flowers, and resins. These ingredients then have to go through another stage of transformation—leaves, flowers, and bark may be dried or placed in oil or water to allow the essential oils to be drawn out; resins are dried or powdered; and then the product can be added to other ingredients or used alone. The power and energy of the original plant is distilled or reduced to a potent compound of its own strength to be used with care and intent.

Obtaining Your Herbs and Oils

When you buy herbs or oils, try to obtain the very best quality, and never use oils that are labelled as "fragrance oils." These are often synthetic, used for room fragrance and not suitable for application to the body, so they may cause a reaction on the skin. Aromatherapy-quality essential oils—those that are extracted from the plant that they are named after—are the best to use and should come in coloured bottles to stop them from degrading. Herbs should be from a reputable supplier and not have been sitting in a jar in the shop for years, as they become stale, dusty, and lose their potency. Store all herbs, oils, and henna in a cool place, out of sunlight and preferably in an airtight container or bottle. Both oils and herbs vary in price; some are particularly expensive, but I shall include substitutes for any that may be prohibitive for some.

Using Herbs and Oils with Power

Both herbs and plant oils have been used for thousands of years and have had various attributes associated with them. Most commonly, they were used to make lotions, unguents, and potions to heal, purify, perfume, or anoint people, animals, and objects. Cosmetics were infused with them; food and drink were flavoured and enhanced by them. Magically, they have always been a major part of the magician's toolkit, used in innumerable ways—whether to anoint body parts, mix into food and drink, add to baths and for ritually washing items, or empower objects such as statues, amulets, and talismans.

A Guide to the Uses of Magical Herbs and Oils

Using herbs and oils in henna magic is simple. When you add the power of herbs, spices, or oils to your henna mix, they need to be in a powdered or liquid form. For example, cinnamon, ginger, or sandalwood can all be obtained as a powder or an oil, but if you have any herbs, spices, or resins that you cannot obtain in a powder or as an essential oil, you will need to crush them into a powder using a mortar and pestle or soak/boil them in water, then strain, to obtain a liquid to mix with your henna. Use the amounts stated in the appropriate spell, and remember that if you are adding powdered herbs or spices to the henna, you may need to add a little more liquid to get the right consistency.

But for now, indulge your senses and find the perfect oil(s) or herb(s) for your recipe. The system is easy; all the herbs and oils are listed by magical goal (listed below). All you need to do is decide on your intent and then choose an oil/herb from the appropriate list to add to your henna recipe.

- Astrological, 114
- Gods & Goddesses, 115
- Happiness, 116
- Healing, 117
- Love, 120
- Planets, 122
- Protection, 123
- Purification, 126
- Spiritual Work, 128
- Wealth & Prosperity, 129

Astrological

Aquarius: Cypress, lavender, patchouli

Aries: Black pepper, ginger, frankincense

Cancer: Chamomile, eucalyptus, lemon, myrrh, palmarosa, yarrow

Capricorn: Benzoin, cypress, patchouli, sandalwood, vetivert

Gemini: Lavender, lemon, lemongrass, peppermint

Leo: Juniper, lime, orange, petigrain, sandalwood

Libra: Cardamom, palmarosa, rose geranium, rose absolute, sandalwood, thyme, ylang-ylang

Pisces: Eucalyptus, lemon, jasmine, sandalwood, ylang-ylang

Sagittarius: Clove, frankincense, myrrh, oakmoss, rosemary

Scorpio: Black pepper, cardamom, galangal, frankincense, pine

Taurus: Benzoin, cardamom, oakmoss, rose, sandalwood, ylang-ylang

Virgo: Cypress, oakmoss, patchouli

Gods & Goddesses

To help attune yourself to or invoke the god or goddess of your choice, use the following oils and herbs:

Aphrodite, Greek goddess of love: Benzoin, rose oil or petals

Apollo, Greek god of the sun: Cypress, frankincense, hyacinth

Buddha: Lotus, plumeria

Demeter, Greek goddess of the harvest: Myrrh, vetivert

Freya, Norse goddess of love: Benzoin, strawberry, rose

Hathor, Egyptian goddess of love: Benzoin

Hecate, Greco-Roman goddess of magic: Lavender, myrrh, vervain (verbena)

Isis, Egyptian goddess of wives, mothers, magic, and nature: Sandalwood, frankincense, myrrh, or rose

Krishna, Hindu supreme god: Basil, lotus

Thoth, Egyptian god of magic: Almond, anise, cinnamon, clove, kyphi, lotus, musk

Triple Goddess, Wiccan Great Goddess (Maiden, Mother, and Crone): Elderberry

Virgin Mary: Rosemary

Zeus, Greek king of the gods: Peppermint, sage, vervain (verbena)

Happiness

Oils

    Apple: Joy

    Cardamom: Warmth, happiness

    Hyacinth: Uplifting

    Lavender: Gentle, harmonious happiness

    Lemon: Get up and go!

    Lime: Uplifting

    Orange: Warming, energetic happiness

    Rose: Soothing, sensual happiness

    Rose Geranium: Balancing

    Ylang-Ylang: Sensual happiness

· ·

Healing

Oils

Cedar: Healing, purifying

Chamomile: Calming, sleep

Comfrey: Healing

Cypress: Healing, comforting

Fennel: Strength, longevity

Geranium: Healing; balancing (especially of hormones)

Jasmine: Healing and general good health; women's ailments (NOTE:
expensive; use ylang-ylang as a substitute or obtain a dilution)

Juniper: Cleansing, good health

Lemon: Cleansing, strengthening

Lemon Balm, Melissa: All healing, protection against illness

Myrrh: Deep healing (spiritual and physical); excellent for skin problems

Peppermint: Good for digestive problems, clears the mind

Pine: Cleansing, healing (NOTE: may irritate sensitive skin)

Rose: Gently healing; good for women and children and for sleep

Rose Geranium: Healing; balances nervous system and adrenals

Rosehip: Good for skin and healing scars

Rosemary: Cleansing, clarifying, good for mental health

Sandalwood: Good for skin, urinary conditions

Spearmint: Good for digestive problems

Tea Tree: Cleansing, deeply healing, good for skin problems, antifungal

Thyme: Relieves dizziness, banishes nightmares

Flowers, Herbs & Powders

Allspice: Healing, warming, good for depression

Cedar: Healing, purifying

Chamomile: Good for sleep, calming

Comfrey: Healing

Cypress: Healing, comforting

Geranium: Healing, balancing

Ginseng: Good health, adaptogen

Goldenseal: Healing, cleansing

Hazel: Good for rheumatism

Hops: Healing, insomnia

Horse Chestnut: Good for aches and pains, circulation

Jasmine Flowers: Healing and general good health, women's ailments

Juniper Berries: Cleansing, good health

Lady's Mantle: Good for women's ailments

Lavender: Balancing, excellent for stress relief

Lemon: Cleansing, strengthening

Magnolia: Hair growth (no guarantees!)

Motherwort: Eases childbirth, strength for women

Mulberry: Eases headaches

Mullein: Eases asthma

Myrrh: Deep healing (spiritual and physical), good for cracked skin

Nettle: Gentle healing, cleansing

Nutmeg: Healing, stimulating, anti-inflammatory

Oak: Longevity

Onion: Use for flu, colds, and lung problems

Peppermint: Good for digestive problems, clears the mind

Pine: Cleansing, healing (NOTE: may irritate sensitive skin)

Rose Geranium: Healing, balances adrenals

Rosehip: Good for skin, heals scars

Rosemary: Cleansing, clarifying, good for mental health

Rose Petals: Gently healing, good for women and children and for sleep

Sage: Longevity

Sandalwood: Good for skin, urinary conditions

Spearmint: Good for digestive problems

Thyme: Relieves dizziness, banishes nightmares

Oils

Cardamom: Intense love, sexuality

Cinnamon: Love, lust (NOTE: may irritate sensitive skin)

Geranium: Love

Jasmine: Promotes attraction

Lavender: Love, chastity

Lemon: Love, friendship

Lemon Balm (known as Melissa): Love

Lemon Verbena (also known as Vervain): Protective love

Orange: Love, harmony, joy

Palmarosa: Sweet love

Patchouli: Lust

Peppermint: Love, lust

Rose: Pure love (NOTE: pure rose oil, known as an absolute, is very expensive, but you can obtain it in a diluted form within a base oil, which is much cheaper while still retaining the scent and energy)

Rosehip: Gentle love

Rosemary: Love, lust, remembrance of love

Vetivert: Love, can also be used to break a love spell put upon you

Ylang-Ylang: Love, lust

Flowers, Herbs & Powders

Balm of Gilead: Mends a broken heart

Cardamom Pods: Intense love and sexuality

Cinnamon: Love, lust (NOTE: may irritate sensitive skin)

Damiana: Love, lust, visions

Dill: Love, lust

Geranium: Love

Ginger: Love, passion

Ginseng: Attracts love

Hibiscus: Love, lust

Lavender: Love, chastity

Lemon Verbena: Love, protection

Mandrake: Powerful love (NOTE: use with extreme caution—very powerful!)

Orange: Love, harmony, joy

Orris Root: Love, attraction, harmonious friendships

Peppermint: Love, lust

Poppy: Love, lust

Raspberry: Protection in love

Rosehip: Gentle love

Rosemary: Love, lust, remembrance of love

Rose petals: Pure love

Strawberry: Love, luck, beauty

Vetivert: Love, can also be used to break a love spell put upon you

Planets

Sun: Acacia, angelica, bay, benzoin, cedar, chamomile, cinnamon, clove, frankincense, juniper, marigold, orange, rosemary, saffron, sandalwood

Moon: Anise, camphor, eucalyptus, honeysuckle, jasmine, lemon, lemon balm, lemongrass, lotus, myrrh, poppy, sandalwood

Mars: Allspice, basil, benzoin, black pepper, galangal, garlic, ginger, peppermint, pine, tobacco

Mercury: Almond, anise, bergamot, cedar, chamomile, dill, lavender, lemongrass, mandrake (NOTE: use with extreme caution—very powerful!), nutmeg, valerian

Jupiter: Anise, balm of gilead, bay, clove, hyssop, sage

Venus: Allspice, almond, balm of gilead, elder (flowers and berries), feverfew, geranium, hibiscus, hyacinth, lavender, orris root, patchouli, rose, rosehips, spearmint, spikenard, vervain, thyme, tonka bean, vervain, vetivert

Saturn: Buckthorn, comfrey, cypress, kava kava, mandrake, patchouli, sage, yarrow, yerba santa

Protection

Oils

Angelica: Protects against evil

Basil: Powerful protection/banishing

Bergamot: Breaks spells

Black Pepper: Potent protection, gives strength (NOTE: may irritate sensitive skin)

Cinnamon: Protection (NOTE: may irritate sensitive skin)

Clove: Protection, exorcising (NOTE: may irritate sensitive skin)

Eucalyptus: Universal oil for protection

Fennel: Wards off evil spirits

Frankincense: Spiritual protection

Juniper: Powerful banishing/purifying

Marigold: Protection in legal or money matters

Myrrh: Protection, transformation, exorcism

Rose Geranium: Protection in love and health

Rosemary: Excellent universal protection

Sandalwood: Powerful spiritual protection

Verbena/Vervain: Protection, purifying

Vetivert: Hex breaking, general protection

Flowers, Herbs & Powders

Acacia: General protection

Angelica: Protects against evil

Anise: Protection

Basil: Powerful protection/banishing

Bay: Protection

Black Pepper: Potent protection, gives strength (NOTE: may irritate sensitive skin)

Blessed Thistle: Protection/spell breaker

Buckthorn: Protection, especially in legal matters

Cedar: Protection, purifying, spell breaker

Cinnamon: Protection (NOTE: may irritate sensitive skin)

Clove: Protection, exorcising (NOTE: may irritate sensitive skin)

Dill: Protects children

Dragon's Blood Resin: Powerful protection and banishing

Elder: Protection, releases spells

Feverfew: Protection from accidents

Frankincense: Spiritual protection

Galangal Root: Protection in legal matters, adds power to spells, spell breaker

Garlic: Powerful banishing, protection, exorcising (NOTE: may have a lingering smell!)

Hyssop: Purifying, protection, banishing

Juniper: Powerful banishing/purifying

Lotus: Protection in love and spirituality

Marigold: Protection in legal or money matters

Myrrh: Protection, transformation, exorcism

Nettle: Spell breaker, protection

Rose Geranium: Protection in love and health

Rosemary: Excellent universal protection

Rowan Wood, Leaves, or Berries: Psychic, magical protection

Rue: Protects against the evil eye, breaks hexes

St. John's Wort: Powerful herb for protection/banishing in general (NOTE: may cause skin sensitivity to sunlight)

Sandalwood: Powerful spiritual protection

Tobacco: Banishing (may be substituted for any herb when used in banishing spells)

Verbena/Vervain: Protection, purifying

Vetivert: Hex breaking, general protection

Walnut: Paralyses evil spirits

Oils

Bay: Mental cleansing

Benzoin: Soothing purification

Cedar: Calmly purifying

Eucalyptus: Universal cleanser and purifier

Frankincense: Spiritual purification

Lavender: Gentle but potent cleansing

Lemon: Physical purification

Lime: Uplifting/reviving purification

Myrrh: Mental, physical, and spiritual purification

Peppermint: Physically purifying, a breath of fresh air

Pine: Deeply cleansing (NOTE: may irritate sensitive skin)

Rosemary: For cleansing negative forces

Sage: Purifying

Sandalwood: Spiritual and mental purification

Flowers, Herbs & Powders

Bay: Mental cleansing

Benzoin: Soothing purification

Camphor: Good for removing negative energies

Chamomile: Gentle cleanser

Eucalyptus: Universal cleanser and purifier

Frankincense: Spiritual purification

Lavender: Gentle but potent cleansing

Lemon: A fresh purifier for mind, body, and spirit

Lime: Uplifting/reviving purification

Myrrh: Mental, physical, and spiritual purification

Peppermint: Physically purifying, a breath of fresh air

Pine: Deeply cleansing (NOTE: may irritate sensitive skin)

Rosemary: Cleansing negative forces

Sandalwood: Spiritual and mental purification

Spiritual Work

Bay: Psychic powers; use in temple ritual

Cinnamon: Astral travel/dream work (NOTE: may irritate sensitive skin)

Frankincense: Use in ritual and for all spiritual/meditation work, initiations

Lemongrass: Visions

Myrhh: For initiations, Wiccan sabbats (festivals)

Nutmeg: Visions

Sandalwood: For sacred spiritual work, initiations, astral travel

Star Anise: Psychic powers

Wealth & Prosperity

Oils

Basil: Wealth

Benzoin Gum: Prosperity

Chamomile: Money, luck

Dill: Money

Ginger: Success, money, power, inspiration

Nutmeg: Luck, money

Oak Moss: Money

Orange: Luck, money

Patchouli: Money

Spearmint: Money, mental powers

Spikenard: Good luck

Tonka Bean: Luck, money, wishes

Vervain: Money

Vetivert: Good luck

Flowers, Herbs & Powders

Allspice: Money, luck

Almond: Prosperity, money

Basil: Wealth

Bayberry: Money, good luck

Benzoin Gum: Prosperity

Buckeye: Money and luck

Cascara: Money, legal matters

Cat's Claw: Money, prosperity

Cedar: Money

Chamomile: Money, luck

Cinquefoil: Wealth, money

Clove: Money

Clover: Money, success, fame

Comfrey: Money

Dill: Money

Ginger: Success, money, power, inspiration

Ginseng: Love and wishes

Goldenseal Root: Money

Honeysuckle: Money

Narcissus: Luck, money

Nutmeg: Luck, money

Oak Moss: Money

Orange: Luck, money

Patchouli: Money

Sassafras: Luck, money

Spearmint: Money, mental powers

Spikenard: Good luck

Tonka Bean: Luck, money, wishes

Vervain: Money

Vetivert: Good luck

Walnut: Tree of Jupiter, good luck, and fortune

Chapter 6

Magical Correspondences

*Draw into yourself all sensations of everything created, fire and water, the dry
and the moist, imagining that you are everywhere, on earth, in the sea, in the sky...
If you embrace in your thought all things at once—all times, places, substances,
qualities, quantities—you may understand God.*
—Hermes Trismegistus

One of the beautiful things about magic is creating the formula for your rituals
and spells. To do this, we can use magical correspondences to bring about an even
more powerful result than pure intent alone. Factors such as the correct time of
day, week, or even year can have an enormous influence on our magical work, so
we need to find out all the corresponding ingredients to create our perfect recipe.

· ·

Let's Start at the Very Beginning...

We all know that our environment affects our emotions, and so putting together
the right correspondences—whether they are elemental, planetary, astrological,
or angelic—strongly affects our magic. All these factors have been used for millennia to empower magical practices, and by using one or all of the appropriate

correspondences, we can make a perfect ritual. If you look at the list of correspondences below, you will notice that they include such things as days of the week, moon phases, colours, numbers, fragrances, tarot cards, Kabbalistic Sephira, and so on. The way to put together the necessary things for your ritual is to choose the ones that appeal to you and that you feel are important and convenient factors to include. You will obviously need to bear in mind where you are going to do your ritual, what you can afford to use, and whether you have the time to dedicate to a long or short process. Rituals can last for minutes or hours, depending on the type of magic and the magician's intent, but it is a purely personal approach. In chapters 8 and 9, there are lists of spells and rituals to use for various purposes, but should you wish to create your very own henna ritual, here is the formula to use.

Constructing a Ritual

Let's say that we want to create a spell to heal ourselves of an ailment. First we can look at the actual condition itself; for our purposes, let's choose something connected with the female reproductive system, such as PMS. We then look at the elements to see which one is associated with this area; the most appropriate would be water—feminine, passive, and with a connection to the planetary sphere of the moon. From here, we can look at the correspondences of the moon and see that it is associated with the colours silver and white, the number nine, Monday, and the angel Gabriel.

So, working on a Monday, you could use nine silver or white candles, or wear something in the appropriate colour such as a robe or silver jewelry. The tarot cards associated with the moon are the High Priestess, the Moon, or the suit of cups, so you may wish to have one of these cards displayed. As the element is water, you could have a small bowl or cup of water available, and should you wish to connect with a deity, you could have an image or statue of one of those listed—for example, Isis or Thoth. You can also include some incense or fragrance—in this case, jasmine, lotus, or camphor. Combined with the oils or herbs categorically listed in chapter 5 and your chosen symbol, you should then be set up to create your very own henna magic!

Moon Phases

The phases of the moon are also an important factor in ritual.

New Moon: Perfect for personal growth, new ventures, and healing.

Waxing Moon: This is when the moon is "growing" and is usually the time for new projects, creations, or principles. Use this time to do magic that invokes attraction, growth, or positive results.

Full Moon: A very fertile time for magic, especially female oriented, protection, or divination spells.

Waning Moon: This is when the moon is fading towards dark and is a very potent time for any magical work that involves banishing negative energy or getting rid of bad habits.

Dark Moon: The last three days of the moon cycle before the new moon; traditionally a time of rest, recuperation, or preparation.

The Correspondences

If you need a reminder as to what correspondences are and how they work, see page 27. Using this information, you can work out which goal and symbol will be best for your henna magic.

- Elemental, 136
- Planetary, 140
- Astrological, 145
- Angelic, 152

Elemental

The four classical elements are crucial to our material and spiritual worldviews; they are the flesh and bones of our systems of magic, the combination of the microcosm and the macrocosm that make up our universe(s), the fundamental principles which structure our world. The universally known four elements of earth, air, fire, and water are shown within many different metaphysical and spiritual schools of thought. The ancient Egyptian creation myths demonstrate the elements as they came into being from the primeval state of chaos and which the students of the god Thoth took as the structure of their magical path, now known as Hermetics. First, there was water, and from this rose a mound of earth; beyond this was the first sunrise (fire), and then came the breath of God (air), and the Word made all things manifest, including the fifth element of spirit.

The early Greek philosophers, including Pythagoras, Plato, and Empedocles, all studied the elemental forms and associated them with the four temperaments (earth—melancholic, air—sanguine, fire—choleric, water—phlegmatic) and the masculine (active) and feminine (passive) principles; later, Aristotle recognized the fifth element of ether (aether), which we recognize as spirit. The alchemists used the four elements in their work and also the philosophical elements of salt, sulphur, and mercury.

EARTH ▽

Passive and feminine, the earth represents the qualities of solidity, firmness, practicality, endurance, perseverance, and material matters, such as wealth and the physical body. Old age and death also come under the auspices of earth.

Gods and Goddesses: Dionysius, Pan, Tammuz, Cernunnos, Demeter, Gaia, Ceres, Bhawana, Mah, Rhea, Persephone

Astrological Signs: Taurus, Virgo, Capricorn

Incense: Benzoin

Moon Phase: New

Direction: North (Northern Hemisphere) or south (Southern Hemisphere)

Alchemical Connections: Salt, lead

Angel: Uriel

Animals: Bull, ox, cow, bison, stag, snake

Finger: Middle

Season: Winter/spring

Time of Day: Midnight

Tarot: The World, suit of pentacles

Positive Traits: Practicality, perseverance, endurance, wisdom

Negative Traits: Stubborn, dull, possessive, greedy, lazy

Body Parts: Bones, legs, sex organs

AIR △

Active and masculine, air is attributed to the mind/mental states but can also represent spirit, as it symbolizes the intermediate level between earth and the spiritual realms. Connected to communication, thought, and logical deduction, air is also representative of intelligence, agility, the imagination, and science. The time of life represented by air is birth.

Gods and Goddesses: Thoth, Shu, Mercury, Khephera, Zeus, Vayu, Arianrhod, Nuit, Urania, Iris, Aditi

Astrological Signs: Gemini, Libra, Aquarius

Incense: Sandalwood

Moon Phase: Waning

Direction: East

Alchemical Connections: Azoth, mercury

Angel: Raphael

Animals: Birds, especially birds of prey

Finger: Index

Season: Spring, winter

Time of Day: Dawn

Tarot: The Fool, suit of swords

Positive Traits: Excitable, optimistic, passionate, logical, just

Negative Traits: Thoughtless, judgmental, critical, impulsive, gullible

Body Parts: Chest, lungs, throat

FIRE △

Active and masculine, fire represents expansion, life force, energy, ambition, and will, as well as spiritual, mystical forces. The time of life attributed to the fire element is youth.

Gods and Goddesses: Vulcan, Horus, Ra, Agni Ea, Prometheus, Bast, Sekhmet, Brigit, Hestia

Astrological Signs: Aries, Leo, Sagittarius

Incense: Olibanum

Moon Phase: Waxing

Direction: South (Northern Hemisphere) or north (Southern Hemisphere)

Alchemical Connections: Sulphur, gold

Angel: Michael

Animals: Lion, horse, dragon

Finger: Little finger

Season: Summer

Time of Day: Noon

Tarot: Judgement, suit of wands

Positive Traits: Creative, expansive, strong willed, ambitious

Negative Traits: Jealous, angry, selfish, restless, feckless

Body Part: Head

WATER ▽

Water is passive and feminine; it governs the emotions and psychological functions. It represents creativity, flow, and love of nature and humankind.

Gods and Goddesses: Neptune, Poseidon, Manannan, Osiris, Aphrodite,
   Tiamat, Mari, Mariamne

Astrological Signs: Cancer, Scorpio, Pisces

Incense: Myrrh

Moon Phase: Full

Direction: West

Alchemical Connections: Mercury, silver

Angel: Gabriel

Animals: Dolphin, fish, sea birds

Finger: Ring

Season: Fall

Time of Day: Sunset

Tarot: Hanged Man, suit of cups

Positive Traits: Loving, connection with others, imaginative

Negative Traits: Depression, instability, indifference, fantastical

Body Parts: Stomach, urinary system

. . . .

Planetary

The planets are a hugely important factor in magical work, for they govern the workings of the astrological signs and have always been believed to have a major influence on the psyche of humans. You can either choose a planet to use that connects with your desired goal or one that resonates with you personally, i.e., corresponds with your astrological sign.

The ancients traditionally only used seven planets (Sun, Moon, Mars, Jupiter, Saturn, Venus, and Mercury), and only when modern technology allowed us to view the more remote planets were they introduced into the magical and astrological sciences. The influence of the more recently discovered planets of Pluto, Neptune, and Uranus are very subtle and evasive forces. As I am a traditionalist (and to avoid confusion), only the original seven planets and their correspondences are included here.

SUN ☉

Colour: Gold/yellow

Day: Sunday

Number: 6

Angel: Michael

Fragrances: Frankincense, cinnamon, kyphi

Gods: Ra, Apollo, Bel, Horus

Goddesses: Bast, Sekhmet

Astrological Sign: Leo

Ritual Uses: Money, honor, promotion, success, gaining support of those in power, friendship, healing, legal matters

Tarot: The Sun, the sixes

Kabbalistic Sephira: Tiphareth, Beauty

MOON ☽

Colours: Silver, white

Day: Monday

Number: 9

Angel: Gabriel

Fragrances: Jasmine, lotus, camphor, ginseng

Gods: Khonsu, Thoth, Anumati

Goddesses: Isis, Hecate, Neith, Diana, Luna, Selene, Artemis

Astrological Sign: Cancer

Ritual Uses: Divination, dreams, visions, love, fertility and travel

Tarot: High Priestess, the nines

Kabbalistic Sephira: Yesod, the Foundation

MERCURY ☿

Colour: Yellow/violet

Day: Wednesday

Number: 8

Angel: Raphael

Fragrance: White sandalwood

Gods: Mercury, Hermes (Thoth), Anubis, Odin

Goddess: Maat

Astrological Signs: Gemini, Virgo

Ritual Uses: General magic, divination and predictions, communication, creativity, intellect, memory

Tarot: The Magician, the eights

Kabbalistic Sephira: Hod, the Glory

VENUS ♀

Colour: Green

Day: Friday

Number: 7

Angel: Anael

Fragrances: Rose, sandalwood, benzoin

Gods: Cupid, Eros, Bes, Adonis, Angus mac Og

Goddesses: Venus, Hathor, Aphrodite, Astarte, Freya, Brigit

Astrological Signs: Taurus, Libra

Ritual Uses: Any magical work that involves love, marriage, and friendship; also the creative arts, drama, and beauty

Tarot: The Empress, the sevens

Kabbalistic Sephira: Netzach, Victory

MARS ♂

Colour: Red

Day: Tuesday

Number: 5

Angel: Samael

Fragrances: Pepper, dragon's blood, tobacco

Gods: Mars, Horus, Ares

Goddesses: Sehkmet, Morrigan, Anath

Astrological Signs: Aries, Scorpio

Ritual Uses: Energy, banishing negative forces, sexual potency/lust, protection, strength

Tarot: The Tower, the fives

Kabbalistic Sephira: Geburah, Severity

JUPITER ♃

Colours: Blue, purple

Day: Thursday

Number: 4

Angel: Sachiel

Fragrances: Saffron, cedar, honeysuckle

Gods: Jupiter, Zeus, Amun, Thor

Goddesses: Maat, Hera, Juno

Astrological Signs: Sagittarius, Pisces

Ritual Uses: Luck, friendship, health, honor, heart's desire

Tarot: Wheel of Fortune, the fours

Kabbalistic Sephira: Chesed, Mercy

SATURN ♄

Colours: Black, brown, grey

Day: Saturday

Number: 3

Angel: Cassiel

Fragrances: Myrrh, cypress, musk

Gods: Saturn, Kronos

Goddesses: Isis, Demeter, Nut, Nepthys

Astrological Signs: Capricorn, Aquarius

Ritual Uses: Business, strengthening responsibility, endings (death/divorce/separations)

Tarot: The World, the threes

Kabbalistic Sephira: Binah, Understanding

Astrological

An astrological sign is a useful symbol to use for work that involves making positive changes to ourselves or for drawing the appropriate energies towards us. Using your own sign as a design for henna can help with overcoming the negative qualities and for strengthening the positive ones. You may also wish to use another sign if you wish to inherit the corresponding qualities or if you are trying to attract a person of that particular astrological sign.

ARIES ♈

March 21–April 20

Symbol: Ram

Element: Fire

Planet: Mars

Gender: Masculine

Colour: Red

Body Parts: Skull, brain, nerve centres

As an Aries, you have great enthusiasm for everything you do and a strong passion for life, with the strength to achieve your goals. Your love of a good challenge includes a real stubborn streak, but this helps you achieve your goals—you know exactly what you want and are not afraid to go for it. However, you often lack patience and can be selfish and uncompromising. Your best matches are Gemini, Leo, Libra, and Scorpio.

TAURUS ☉

April 21–May 21

Symbol: Bull

Element: Earth

Planet: Venus

Gender: Feminine

Colour: Green

Body Parts: Throat and neck area

Taureans tend to be practical, calm, and reliable, with a sensual yet determined nature. Like its opposite sign of Scorpio, Taurus is a very sexual sign. Negative traits include hedonism, laziness, and jealousy. The best romantic partners for Taurus would be Libra, Scorpio, and Capricorn.

GEMINI ♊

May 22–June 21

Symbol: The twins

Element: Air

Planet: Mercury

Gender: Masculine

Colour: Yellow

Body Parts: The upper torso, related organs, arms

If you are born under the sign of Gemini, you can expect to be the lord/lady of communication, whether physical, mental, or spiritual. Airy and mercurial,

Gemini has no problem expressing ideas but often finds decision making difficult. Fun-loving and sociable, Gemini may have a darker side that is moody, unreliable, and superficial. Gemini will get on best with Virgo, Libra, and Sagittarius folk.

CANCER ♋

June 22–July 22

Symbol: Crab

Element: Water

Planet: Moon

Gender: Feminine

Colour: Brown

Body Parts: Breasts, digestive organs, womb

Cancer people are vulnerable and emotional; often the world is a scary place for them to be, and they prefer the safety of their home and domesticity. This, however, makes them peacemakers—nurturing, kind, and intuitive, with a definite romantic side. The downside of this is general moodiness, depression, and changeability. The best allies for Cancerians are Pisces, Scorpio, and Aquarius.

LEO ♌

July 23–August 23

Symbol: Lion

Element: Fire

Planet: Sun

Gender: Masculine

Colour: Gold

Body Parts: Heart, spine, back

Egotistical Leo has a huge love of life, creativity, and drama and adores being the center of attention. Leo is proud, enthusiastic, honest, and warm-hearted, but can also be self-centred, materialistic, and arrogant. Romantic encounters are best with Scorpio, Capricorn, or fellow Leos.

VIRGO ♍

August 24–September 22

Symbol: The Virgin

Element: Earth

Planet: Mercury

Gender: Feminine

Colour: Orange

Body Parts: Large and small intestine, spleen and pancreas, hands and nails

Virgo is the intelligent, self-sufficient, and methodical one who is modest, controlled, and organized but can spill over into fussiness, hypochondria, and cold perfectionism. However, Virgos are excellent at analyzing facts and make exceptional detectives! Compatible friends include Gemini, Pisces, or Taurus.

LIBRA ♎

September 23–October 22

Symbol: Scales

Element: Air

Planet: Venus

Gender: Masculine

Colour: White

Body Parts: Lumbar region, buttocks, excretory organs

The sign of Libra is the scales or "balance" that embodies the very thing Librans stand for: justice and balance. Highly intelligent, charming, and idealistic, Libra's darker side is one of cruelty, greed, envy, and anger. They make very good friends for all astrological signs but particularly Aries, Aquarius, and Taurus when it comes to love.

SCORPIO ♏

October 23–November 21

Symbol: Scorpion

Element: Water

Planet: Mars (traditional), Pluto (modern)

Gender: Feminine

Colour: Black

Body Parts: Pelvis, reproductive organs, kidneys

Intense, passionate, and powerful Scorpio! Analytical, highly perceptive, and self-contained, Scorpio can also be cruel, jealous, and cunning. Hypnotically sensual and alluring, Scorpios need to be aware of their intensity when it comes to all things sexual, for they are prone to all-consuming passion and have a self-destructive element. However, they make exciting lovers and blend well with Capricorn, Pisces, and Leo.

SAGITTARIUS ♐

November 22–December 21

Symbol: The Archer

Element: Fire

Planet: Jupiter

Gender: Masculine

Colour: Blue

Body Parts: Hips, thighs, sacrum

Sagittarian types are philosophical and broadminded but often become dissatisfied and bored quickly. They are usually energetic and dynamic, which makes travel and adventure appealing. They are compassionate and stand for justice and morality. On the downside, Sagittarians can be a bit too honest for some people, with exacting standards and a tendency to be unreasonable and unable to learn from their mistakes. In love, Sagittarius works well with Gemini, Aries, Taurus, and Virgo.

CAPRICORN ♑

December 22–January 20

Symbol: Goat

Element: Earth

Planet: Saturn

Gender: Feminine

Colour: Grey

Body Parts: Bones, skin

The "horned goat" is probably the most serious and businesslike of the zodiac. Practical, responsible, and with a superb work ethic, Capricorns are ambitious and shrewd in all that they do, which can make them somewhat dull, stubborn, cold, and rigid in personality. However, they are intensely protective of loved ones, which often include Taurus, Scorpio, and Leo.

AQUARIUS ≈

January 21–February 19

Symbol: Water Bearer

Element: Air

Planet: Saturn (traditional), Uranus (modern)

Gender: Masculine

Colour: Blue/green

Body Parts: Lower leg, circulatory system

Aquarians are the rebels of the zodiac, with great energy and enthusiasm for independence and unusual ideas. Usually dependable and very honest, they can be relied upon to be considerate to others but equally can be erratic and changeable due to their dual nature. They get along well with other Aquarians or those under the signs of Gemini, Libra, and Pisces.

PISCES ♓

February 20–March 20

Symbol: Fish

Element: Water

Planet: Jupiter (traditional), Neptune (modern)

Gender: Feminine

Colour: Purple

Body Parts: Feet, ankles, lymphatic system

Sensitive Pisces is often perceived as a victim of life due to their ability to act as a sponge to everything good, bad, or indifferent. Highly emotional, sensitive, and passionate, Pisceans tend to be compassionate and helpful to others. However, this overwhelming emotional state can lead to an excess of dreaminess, unreality, and paranoia. They make good friends and intense lovers, especially with Aquarius, Cancer, and Scorpio people.

* *

Angelic

Using the forces of the archangels is an ancient form of magic and one that many people feel very comfortable with. The seven angels represent many different aspects, but the main ones are listed below for use in your henna work, including the day and hours ruled by each angel. This can be of use for those wishing to work their magic at the appropriate time of day or night. In occult lore, the day begins at sunrise (not at midnight), and the night begins at the thirteenth hour after sunrise.

MICHAEL

Planet: Sun

Day: Sunday

Time: First and eighth hour of day, third and tenth hour of night

Ritual Colour: Golden yellow

Symbol: Hexagram

Magical Influences: Ambition, success, business, new jobs, growth, expansion. Peace, hope, prosperity. Magic to influence friendships, health (mental and physical), and money, and to bring light and joy into your life. Also beneficial for banishing dark or negative influences.

GABRIEL

Planet: Moon

Day: Monday

Time: First and eighth hour of day, third and tenth hour of night

Ritual Colour: White or silver

Symbol: Nine-pointed star

Magical Influences: Emotional issues, feminine mysteries and fertility, psychic ability and dreams. Marriage, domestic life, family, travel, and medicine. Useful for influencing the outcome or protection of journeys, dreams, or goals, and for magical work involving clairvoyance and prophecy.

SAMAEL

Planet: Mars

Day: Tuesday

Time: First and eighth hour of day, third and tenth hour of night

Ritual Colour: Red

Symbol: Five-pointed star

Magical Influences: Masculine energy. Physical strength and courage, especially to help overcome enemies or obstacles. Vitality, assertiveness, and competitiveness. Useful for banishing negative influences and for magic to protect when undergoing surgery.

RAPHAEL

Planet: Mercury

Day: Wednesday

Time: First and eighth hour of day, third and tenth hour of night

Ritual Colour: Yellow

Symbol: Eight-pointed star

Magical Influences: Success in business, communication, and mental abilities. Excellent for creative projects such as writing, drama, poetry, and science, and influences all forms of study, learning, and teaching. Also very useful for inspirational or self-improvement work. Protects during travel and is also useful for healing.

SACHIEL

Planet: Jupiter

Day: Thursday

Time: First and eighth hour of day, third and tenth hour of night

Ritual Colour: Purple

Symbol: Square

Magical Influences: General health, wealth, and ambition. Social status, friendships, and legal issues. Excellent for work involving finances, success, or luck.

ANAEL

Planet: Venus

Day: Friday

Time: First and eighth hour of day, third and tenth hour of night

Ritual Colour: Green

Symbol: Seven-pointed star

Magical Influences: Any work involving love, friendship, romance, marriage, physical beauty, fertility, and sexual matters. Influences the pursuit of sensuality, the arts, music, luxury, pleasure, and comfort.

CASSIEL

Planet: Saturn

Day: Saturday

Time: First and eighth hour of day, third and tenth hour of night

Ritual Colour: Black, brown, grey

Symbol: Straight line

Magical Influences: Karma, reincarnation, karmic lessons, mysteries, and wisdom. Old age, the passage of time, death, and banishing and removal of spirits or disease. Spirit manifestation/communication, meditation, protection against psychic attack. The finding of lost objects or missing people. Homes, buildings, boundaries, and anything involving authorities.

Contemporary "Bollywood,"
or hybrid-style, henna

Chapter 7

A Henna Ritual: The Application

Henna paste is going to be applied, it will stain my hands red.
My friends say, now flower buds are going to blossom in your hands.
Your heart, your life are going to receive new joys.
—Mehndi Hai Rachnewali, from the film *Zubeidaa*

The application of henna is a ritual in itself; preparation, taking time, and the meditative process of applying the design all make for a very special and sacred experience. You can't hurry henna; it is a magical substance in itself, creating an alchemical change from powder to liquid to its deep, rich stain. It makes its mark, holds its essence, but cannot be hurried, for haste will produce inferior magic.

· ·

Types of Henna

There are several countries that export henna powder either for use as a hair dye or for body decoration. It is advisable to buy your henna powder from a supplier who specializes in body-art quality (BAQ) henna; they themselves will have bought a very good, fresh supply direct from a reputable supplier in the country of origin. Henna bought from health stores or ethnic food stores may have been sitting on

the shelves or exposed to the light for a long time, and henna loses its dyeing properties once it has become stale. Fresh henna powder is light green and mixes to a brown paste; stale henna will be a dull green/brown. Be cautious of bright green powder, as it may be old henna that has been freshened up with green dye.

Listed below are the various products that can be classed as "henna," some of which are positively dangerous—it is a good thing to become acquainted with what is available. Please refer to the coloured endpages for visual examples of different hennas.

> *Neutral Henna:* Technically, there is no such thing as "neutral" henna, but what you will be getting is *Cassia obovata* (*Senna* genus), a green powder that has no actual henna added and is purely a simple but superb conditioning treatment for hair and nails.

> *Red Henna or Traditional Henna (Lawsonia inermis):* Made using henna leaf buds, which contain a strong tannin concentration, giving it the characteristic red tone. This is a light green powder that mixes to deep reddish-brown paste; the resulting stain depends on the area the henna comes from.

> North African henna such as Moroccan and Yemeni make a stringier paste that helps give a fine, strong line and produces a warm, deep red stain. Persian henna is reputed to produce a darker red stain, whereas Indian henna is believed to give a more brownish-red hue. However, it is more likely the variation in colour is due to application methods and/or the type of skin the henna is applied to, as each person's chemical makeup is different, and this can affect the final result.

> *Indigo or Victorian Black Henna (Indigofera tinctoria):* Note that this is *not* PPD "black henna"—in India or the Middle East, indigo was used

with or after applying red henna to achieve a blue-black tone. Indigo has a distinct colour to it and is distinguishable from imitation black hennas by its blueness when mixed. Other so-called black henna powders may have crushed walnut or oak gall added; to be on the safe side, always conduct a small skin-patch test to check for any irritation these ingredients may cause. Indigo may be used on the skin as a temporary stain, which can range from a sensuously dark inky blue to a moody grey.

Black Henna: There is actually no such thing as "black" henna; if you do see henna specified as black, it will invariably have something added, usually a chemical dye. If it comes from a Middle Eastern or Indian shop, it may be henna mixed with indigo or other colourings; however, if it is sold in a clear tube or as a black- or coffee-coloured powder, then it is very likely to be fake "black henna" and is to be avoided at all costs. This substance contains PPD (paraphenylenediamine), which is normally used in commercial hair dye but is not approved for direct use on the skin, and it is either sold as a paste or mixed with henna powder, which gives off a black liquid stain and can smell similar to frozen peas. If you go on holiday and are offered a "henna tattoo," be very careful as to what you are allowing on your skin; it is unlikely to be ordinary henna. Please do not use this product or allow anyone you know to have a "black henna" tattoo, as it may cause severe skin damage and a permanent allergic reaction to PPD dyes in future.

There are several nontoxic alternatives to black henna called *harquus* and *jagua*, which can be used to achieve a black temporary tattoo and are FDA approved; although not henna-based, should you be desperate for a black design, they can be obtained from the suppliers listed at the back of the book. Both harquus and jagua have been used for centuries.

An example of a henna kit including a tube of henna, oil, and stencils. To use stencils, place on a clean, dry hand, cover with henna paste, leave until dry, and then remove the stencil. Protect the design with wrappings for several hours (preferably overnight), then remove any dried henna and rub in the oil to bring out the colour.

Harquus is the name used for the black facial adornments of the North African and Middle Eastern cultures, incorporating both tattooing and body painting, which were often used in conjunction with henna as a complementary decoration. You can obtain harquus from mehandi.com (see appendix). Jagua is a natural black dye from a South American plant and has been used by tribal people for centuries. It gives a blue-grey or blue-black stain and lasts for around ten to fifteen days.

Henna comes in several forms—most notably a green powder (consisting of the dried, crushed leaves) that, when mixed with liquid, resembles a brownish-red mud. It has a distinctive herby or grassy smell and stains the skin almost immediately. To achieve a perfect design, you will need to obtain fresh henna that has *not* been sitting on a shelf for the past five years! The suppliers at the back of the book are meticulous about their stock and will only sell fresh, well-sifted henna. Fresh henna powder is a strong green and will produce a deep brownish-red mix; stale henna will be a dull green, turning brownish when mixed, and will produce inferior staining. For your designs, you will need very finely sifted powder, free from the twigs and general debris sometimes found in the henna used for dyeing hair. This is available as body-art quality (BAQ) henna from the stockists listed in the appendix; if you do buy elsewhere and find that it is a bit twiggy, you can sift your powder by putting a nylon stocking or piece of pantyhose over a cup and gently sieving the henna through it.

Henna is also available in freshly made paste, either in a bag, a tub, or filled cones. These can be bought from a good supplier who will make a fresh paste and send them to you so that you can use them immediately or store them in the freezer until you need them; they should last several months. You may also find tubes of henna in Indian stores, but do check that they are not old and dusty, as the henna will most likely be stale and offer little or no staining power.

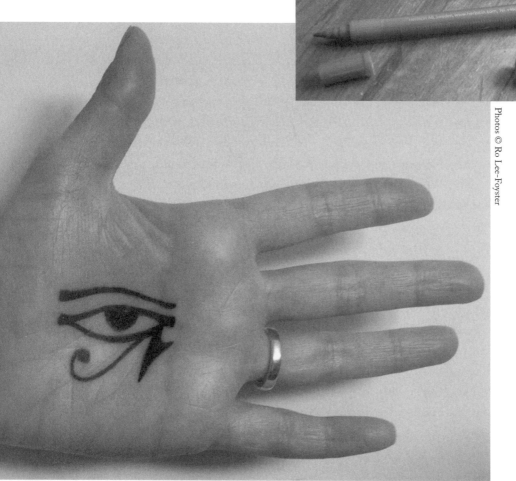

The Henna Penna, right, and an example design using the Henna Penna, below

A new product is available called Henna Penna. It is a pen filled with liquid henna that you can use quite literally to draw designs on your body. It is marketed as having no artificial additives or colours, is not tested on animals, and has a double nib for ease of use. I find it very easy to use, and it gives a remarkably good stain, but only for a few days; while it is definitely not as pleasurable as mixing your own henna, it is useful for quick designs (see appendix).

How Does Henna Stain, and How Long Will It Last?

Henna stains the skin on contact; it is an amazing dye, and even if left on for just a minute there will be a noticeable change in colour. The depth of stain, however, will vary from person to person, as will the recipe and method used for mixing and the type of henna used. The areas on the body that stain darkest and longest are those which have thicker skin, such as the soles of the feet, the palms of the hands, fingers, and toes. The areas that stain lighter shades are where the skin is thinner, such as the backs of the hands, the tops of the feet, arms, legs, back, and chest. Areas that exfoliate quicker are also more susceptible to lesser staining power. It can also depend on your body temperature or metabolism, and whether your skin is acidic or alkaline, as to whether you will get a stain anywhere between pale orange to a deep red or purplish black. The chart located on the colour page in the back gives an indication of the variety of shades that can occur from henna dye.

When making your potion, you can achieve a better and deeper colour by using a mordant. This is a substance that brings out and fixes the dye in the henna and intensifies the colour, making it longer lasting. These ingredients are high in terpene, which is a chemical in the plant that makes them a powerful mordant, and

*Mordants, or ingredients used to help release
the dye in the henna, include lemon juice,
essential oils, coffee, cloves, etc.*

they are used in the process called *terping*, where the henna paste is left to stand, often for many hours, to release the dye.

The most common mordants are:

Citrus Fruits: Lemons, limes, or grapefruit

Essential Oils: Eucalyptus, tea tree, camphor, pine, cajeput, frankincense, ravensara, geranium, lavender, lemon, lime, grapefruit

Spices, Herbs, or Juices: Coffee, tea, cloves, fenugreek, paprika, pomegranate juice, cardamom

These ingredients are often experimental, and I would only use one or two at a time. Some of the oils can be irritating to the skin and must be used with caution. I always recommend doing a small patch test with any mixture, either discreetly just behind the ear or in the crook of the elbow, leaving the patch to develop over twenty-four hours. This should give adequate time to demonstrate any adverse reaction. If you have very sensitive skin, it is probably best to avoid everything except maybe the lemon juice.

Making a good henna paste is often a case of trial and error, and it is fun to experiment with different quantities and types of ingredients. You will need to play around with developing times for the paste—some henna powder, such as Moroccan henna, releases its dye very quickly, but others may need varying standing times. Part of the beauty of henna decoration is the time and effort put into it; it is definitely not a process to be rushed and can become a deeply meditative pastime.

Getting Started

Firstly, a few precautions:

Henna and Children: Do *not* use henna on children under five, as its use for large applications (e.g., palm, head, etc.) has been linked to blood cell depletion leading to hyperbilirubinemia. In the case of children with G6PD (glucose-6-phosphate dehydrogenase) deficiency, henna can cause serious risk of illness or death and should be avoided.

Henna and Pregnancy: Although henna is generally believed to be safe to use during pregnancy, it is always worth asking a healthcare professional for advice. If you have had any previous problems with sensitivity to henna, then it is probably wise to avoid its use—and this applies to pregnant women who are applying henna as well.

    Always remember that essential oils should not be used during the first three months of pregnancy, and for the second and third trimesters only use those that are safe for application during this time. Avoid lying on your back, as it can be uncomfortable and you may not be able to adjust your posture adequately with a belly covered in henna. Sitting upright, propped up with cushions, will probably be the most comfortable position. Henna has been used ritually to celebrate the growing life and the joys of pregnancy for many hundreds of years, and it is considered to be a safe and beautiful practice.

Henna Quality: Make sure that the henna you buy is of the highest quality—preferably organic if you can find it. Unfortunately, some manufacturers are still adding illegal or dangerous substances to henna powder either to give it a better colour or to cover up the use of stale powder. Bearing in

mind that henna application will need to remain on the skin for anywhere between one and twenty-four hours, you should only expose yourself to a pure product. Never use henna that is packaged or labeled as hair dye or is classed as compound henna (unless it states that it is body-art quality henna), as this can contain anything from metallic salts to PPD and cannot be guaranteed safe for skin use.

Essential Oils: When using essential oils either to strengthen the colour or as a magical correspondence, always use aromatherapy-grade oils only— do not use oils classed as fragrance oils, such as those often sold with oil burners, as these are often synthetic and may cause skin irritation. In chapter 8, I list various oils in the recipes that correspond with the desired result.

Sensitive Skin: Henna application for those with sensitive skin should be carefully done—the lemon juice and/or essential oils may be too strong and cause a reaction. Use caution and experiment gently to find a suitable mix. Please use your common sense and apply a small skin-patch test before doing any large designs.

Storing Your Henna: Store your henna in an airtight container—you can use plastic tubs, zipper resealable plastic bags like Ziploc, or a good screw-top glass jar—and keep it away from direct sunlight. Premixed henna paste or good-quality fresh henna powder can be stored in the fridge or freezer. If freezing, make up small batches using plastic bags, bottles, or cones, which can be defrosted as required. Henna should remain good for several months in the freezer or several days in the fridge without losing its staining power.

*Equipment for
applying henna*

Equipment

Here is what you will need for henna mixing and application:

- Finely sifted henna
- Cones, carrot or frosting bags, and/or a jacquard bottle and metal tips
- Essential oils—aromatherapy-grade oils only
- Lemon juice (strained if fresh, but bottled is just as effective)
- Cloves, tea, coffee, etc.
- Sugar
- A pair of plastic or latex gloves
- A glass bowl
- A saucepan to heat up any spices or tea/coffee you are using

Cones, Bottles, and Brushes

You will also need to choose a method of applying the paste. There are several different methods used around the world; in India, they tend to use a cone (a bit like a cake frosting bag). These are usually made from Mylar, or plastic, tissue or florists' cellophane, which you can buy in sheet form or ready-made as a cone from many of the stockists listed at the back of the book. They are fairly simple to make once you have your plastic.

You will need:

- Cellophane/Mylar
- Scissors
- Scalpel or craft knife
- Cutting board or similar
- Sticky tape

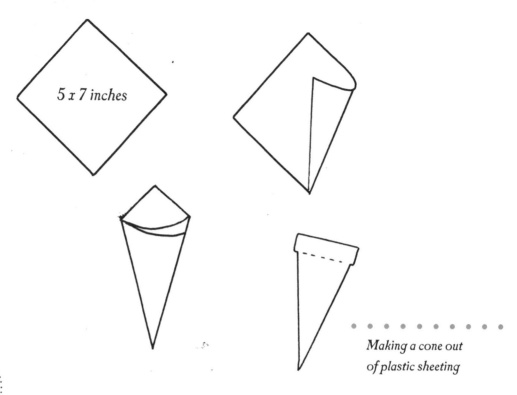

5 x 7 inches

Making a cone out of plastic sheeting

Cut the plastic into 5 x 7-inch rectangles and then take the right corner and fold it back to the middle to create the point of the cone (see above, top right). Roll the cone until you get the right width, then roll over the flat sheet to your left to make a complete cone, adjusting the shape until you get a suitable point. Once you are satisfied with the shape, tape down the "tail" corner left over near the tip of the cone. You can also tape along the point so that it keeps its shape and add two more bits of tape along the length of the cone. For instructions on filling your cone, see page 175.

Also available are carrot bags, which are very similar to cake-decorating bags and are brilliant to use for filling cones and bottles. I have found they are pretty good for applying henna as well; all you need to do is fill the bag with henna paste, tie just above the line of the henna, and snip a tiny piece off the end of the cone. Be cautious about cutting the hole, as it is always easier to cut a bit at a time than end up cutting too much off and finding that your henna pours out. The bag can then be held like a pen or in the fist, whichever is easier and more comfortable, and squeezed gently to produce a fine stream of paste.

In Morocco, the *seqaasha* (henna painters) use a syringe with the point of the needle taken off to produce a blunt nib. In Tunisia, a stick is used, similar to that used to apply kohl to the eyes. Modern Western henna artists tend to favor the cone or what is known as a jacquard bottle. Commonly used for silk painting, it is a plastic bottle with a long nozzle or metal nib and is widely available from craft shops or via the Internet; the metal nibs come in various sizes to allow a choice of thickness for the lines of the design. The bottle is simple to use but will need some practice, and for large designs a cone may be more comfortable to squeeze.

You could even experiment using a paintbrush. This is not a method for purists but would be fun to try if you don't feel confident using the cone or bottle at first.

The choice of application is a matter of trial and error, and I would recommend trying them all to see which one you are most comfortable with and which also produces the best results.

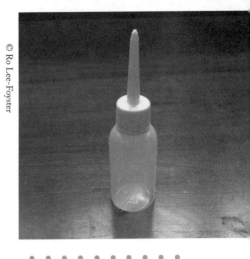

A bottle is simplest to use but will require some practice

Henna Recipes
A Step-by-Step Guide to Mixing Your Paste

There are literally hundreds of different recipes for making henna paste from all around the globe, some of which are closely guarded secrets, but below are some simple recipes that should produce a good paste. Some experimentation is often necessary, and it is a good idea to do a very small patch test to determine colour and/or any skin irritation that may rarely occur. The beauty of preparing the henna paste is that you can continue to add your own little touches to find out what works best for you. Henna may differ with each batch, depending on where your henna comes from and how it is treated, so the colour and consistency of the powder may vary.

The henna powder needs to release its dye, and this can take a number of hours but can also be helped along by adding the various mordants mentioned previously.

Make sure you have obtained finely sifted fresh henna; see the stockists at the back of the book so that you can be assured of the finest quality henna. If the henna is not fresh, it will not stain well, so ensure that you buy some that is from a recent crop. If you do need to sift the henna to remove any debris such as stalks, bits of leaves, etc., use an old stocking wrapped over a cup or glass. Put a table-spoon of henna at a time on top of the stocking, and gently shake or stir the powder so that it falls through into the glass; when you have the required amount, carefully remove the stocking and tip the sifted henna into a bowl. Using a plastic or glass bowl is preferable to a metal one, as sometimes the lemon juice in the mix can react and either tarnish the bowl or leach metal into the henna paste.

Really Simple Henna Paste

This is a good starter recipe, as it is easy to get the right consistency and volume, and it is also suitable for those with sensitive skin. The sugar gives the paste a good consistency and helps it to flow from the applicator. It also slows down the drying rate and therefore should prevent cracking. The lemon juice alters the pH balance of the henna, assisting in the darkening process. This particular method is also good if you just want to add specific corresponding zodiacal, elemental, or magical oils, as the ingredients will not clash with other oils and the fragrance should be pleasant and quite noticeable.

This gives enough paste for one large design or several small ones. If you wish to double up on quantity, you can always freeze some (good for several months) or put some in the fridge (good for several days). To freeze your henna, either scoop it into a plastic bottle, plastic bag, or cone; you may wish to double-bag it if you are worried it might leak. When defrosting your henna, pop it into a small jug of hot water until it softens, and then leave it to cool before applying it to the skin.

Ingredients

- 2 tablespoons finely sifted henna
- Strained juice of 1 large lemon or 2–4 tablespoons bottled juice
- 1 teaspoon sugar

To Mix

Add henna powder and sugar to a glass or ceramic bowl (avoid a plastic bowl, as it will stain, unless you are going to use it regularly for henna), and add some of the lemon juice. Mix the powder, adding liquid as necessary, until you get a whipped cream consistency that is completely mixed, with no dry pockets of powder.

Photos © Ro Lee-Foyster

• • • • • • • • • •

Mixing the paste, top;
covered paste left to develop, above;
and filling the cone, right

Note: now is the time to add any herb, spice, powder, liquid, or oil if you are doing a specific spell. But if you just need a basic paste, carry on . . .

When you are happy with the feel of the mix, cover the bowl with cling wrap and leave in a warm place for six to twenty-four hours.

When the dye has released, scoop the henna into a bottle or cone. The release of dye can be checked by uncovering the bowl and checking for a brown layer on the top of the paste; if you scoop off this layer, the greenish paste will show underneath. Alternatively, if you already have put your henna into a plastic cone or bag, lay a piece of kitchen paper, or a paper towel, underneath the plastic, and when the dye has released there will be a slight orangeish stain on it where the dye has seeped through the bag or cone.

How to Fill Your Cone or Bottle

Placing the empty cone in a glass or cup helps keep the cone upright and will allow you to use both hands while filling. Fill the cone roughly one-half to three-quarters full with the henna paste, which is approximately 2–3 tablespoons.

Holding the filled cone in one hand, with the other hand gather the plastic at the open end and carefully twist it just above the level of the paste. Securely wrap a rubber band around it, fold over the end, and tape it down. To allow the paste to flow out the end of the cone, cut a tiny piece off the tip—don't cut much to begin with, as it is often easy to overestimate how big a hole you will need, and you may end up with a "whoosh" of henna flooding out (which is then impossible to rectify, and you will have wasted a cone). Test the rate of flow on a piece of paper, and if necessary snip a small amount off again.

To fill your bottle, scoop or squirt the paste into the bottle using a spoon or filled cone. If you want to be safe, pop the bottle into a glass to catch any spills or stop it from falling over.

Terpene-Rich Henna Paste

Note: You will need to premix this paste at least a day before you need to apply the henna (unless you are making a batch to freeze), as it can take 24–48 hours for the dye to fully develop.

This mixture contains the terpene-rich essential oils or spices that really bring out the colour, but it should only be used for those without sensitive skin.

If you are doing a spell or charm using corresponding oils, see if there are some that are in the mordant list (see page 165); if not, it may be better to use the really simple henna paste recipe on page 173 to avoid wrong correspondences—or a revolting fragrance!

Ingredients

- 2–3 tablespoons finely sifted henna
- 1 teaspoon sugar or honey

Here comes the alchemy…experiment and create your own magical brew! All these ingredients are either sugars, acids, tannins, or plant dyes and can improve the colour and consistency of your paste. Do remember that if you add more powder to the henna, the liquid ratio will need to be increased, and vice versa. The resulting paste needs to be the consistency of thick whipped cream, so use your judgment and add powder/liquid as necessary. The beauty of making the paste is that it is a magical process in itself—use your intuition and just play with the various ingredients until you get the best paste and the best stain.

You can add any or several of these to your henna and sugar:

- Lemon, grapefruit, or lime juice
- Tamarind paste
- Pomegranate juice or syrup

- Coffee or black tea, brewed for several hours or overnight
- Cardomom, powdered
- Cloves steeped in tea or water and simmered until you get a nice strong liquid
- Red wine
- Vinegar
- Hibiscus tea
- Ginger, fresh or powdered (if using fresh ginger, simmer in water for an hour and strain)
- Paprika
- Citric acid
- Flowers, herbs, and powders for ritual use (see chapter 5)

Adding the
essential oil

When you have mixed your paste, cover the bowl with cling wrap and leave for several hours. After 4–8 hours, you can add your essential oils for terping or ritual use (see chapter 5).

Add the essential oils—5–10 drops per tablespoon of paste—mix well, cover the bowl, and leave for a further 12 or so hours. To try the staining power of the paste, you can always dab a spot on your palm and leave it for a minute to see if it gives an immediate stain. You can then proceed with filling your cone or bag.

The following henna paste recipe is from expert henna artist Farah Khan.

A full arm design by
expert henna artist
Farah Khan

Farah's Recipe

There are hundreds of different variations of henna paste recipes in the world. This is one of my favorites. It makes good sense to source a very good quality super-sifted powder (Jamila is excellent) that comes from a recent crop. The powder should not have any bark or bits in it, but you may need to sift it yourself a couple of times. It should appear very fine.

Ingredients

- 20 grams or ¼ cup henna powder
- ½ cup lemon juice
- ½ cup black tea
- Clove oil (optional; omit if you have very sensitive skin or are going to use magical essential oils)
- Eucalyptus oil (optional; omit if you have very sensitive skin or are going to use magical essential oils)

Initially, you should mix half a cup of brewed black tea (left for ten hours) with the same amount of freshly squeezed lemon juice. Then add this mixture to the sieved henna and leave up to three hours. It should be the consistency of custard or icing sugar—just slowly add more lemon juice to get to that state. After about five hours, the henna should be ready. Just before you cone up, add seven drops of clove oil and seven of eucalyptus oil and mix well.

Lemon and Sugar Glaze

Last but not least, when you have finished your design, you need to fix it with a lemon and sugar glaze. This will help preserve the decoration by keeping the henna on the skin and will also bring out the colour even more.

Ingredients

- 1 teaspoon sugar
- 2 teaspoons lemon juice

Add the two ingredients together, stir to dissolve the sugar, and use as needed. To apply, dab the glaze onto the skin with a cotton ball or tissue.

There is also a product called New-Skin that creates a breathable, protective layer on the skin and is normally used for keeping wounds clean; however, it is also useful for covering dried henna designs.[15]

15 See http://www.newskinproducts.com/

Applying Your Design
A Step-by-Step Guide

Preparing the Skin for Decoration

You will need to make sure that the area of skin you wish to decorate is free from any oil, lotions, or other substances and has been exfoliated to remove any rough skin. You can either wash the area you are going to henna thoroughly using plain soap and water or use an alcohol wipe or lemon juice to remove any traces.

It helps to be warm when you have a henna decoration applied—heat is a great helper in the development of the colour. Make yourself and/or the person you are decorating a big cup of hot tea; put the heat on or sit outside and allow the heat of the sun to do its stuff. In Morocco and other areas, the area of the body being decorated is often exposed to braziers of hot coals to really bring out the colour. Obviously, do be sensible and don't allow your feet or hands to get too close to a heat source; if outside in the sun, protect yourself with a parasol or sit in the shade to avoid giving yourself sunburn or heatstroke. It may also be a good idea to time your henna session in the evening; that way, you can cover your design and then go to bed. The warmth from being tucked up will allow the henna to work its magic overnight, and you will end up with a beautiful, rich colour.

Have Everything You Need at Hand

The decorating process should be a relaxed and pleasant pastime, and the last thing you need is to keep having to dash around looking for ingredients or equipment. Also, if you are working on yourself, you will not be able to move around too much, depending on where the design is placed. You will need to be sitting comfortably, whether you are decorating or being decorated. The application and drying process can be slow, depending on the size of the design. If you are having your feet done,

Creating a ritual environment

you will have to stay still for quite some time, otherwise you may end up trailing henna through the house. Similarly, if you are decorating your hands, you may not be able to pick up or hold anything until the design is dry. If you are in a rush or are impatient to get on, you can use a hair dryer to speed up the drying process, and then cover the design with tissue or gauze, tape it up, and pop on some cotton gloves or socks. However, it is wonderful to make the experience as enjoyable as possible, so light some candles, put on some music or a favorite movie, and even pour a glass of wine. If you wish to make it even more special, use the time to create a ritual environment using your own special objects such as corresponding incense, candles, and colours, etc.

Do be aware that henna can stain *everything*! Don't settle down to apply henna on your lovely cream sofa—an errant blob of mixture will be a disaster, and bits of the henna may flake off during the drying process. Make sure that any fabrics or furnishings are covered with a plastic sheet and a towel or two.

Equipment

You will need:

- Cone, bag, or bottle filled with henna paste
- Thin latex gloves
- Toilet tissue
- Cotton buds (to wipe off any errors—but be quick, henna stains rapidly!)
- Toothpicks (to help with any intricate dots of henna that need applying)
- Tiger Balm ointment (has essential oils in it that help bring out the design after the henna is removed; optional—may cause irritation to sensitive skin)
- Surgical tape

- Kitchen paper/tissues
- Cotton wool pads
- Alcohol wipes
- Lemon and sugar glaze fixative
- New-Skin liquid (can be used in place of the lemon and sugar, as it creates a moisture-proof barrier over the dried henna)
- Gauze/cotton glove or sock (to cover and protect the dried design; available from pharmacies)
- Hot water bottle or heating pad (optional—may be used to apply heat directly to the covered design, which helps bring out the colour)

How to Use a Bottle or Cone

One of the great things about the popularity of using henna means that we can use the wisdom of others to practice our art. Modernly, there are lots of ways to make the process simpler, and one of these is the jacquard bottle. Originally used for silk painting, these squeezy plastic bottles are fitted with stainless steel tips that are available from craft suppliers in three sizes, giving you the ability to create very small, delicate lines or bolder lines for filling in. A gentle pressure on the bottle produces a perfect and consistently even line of henna, so they are especially suitable for beginners, as they do not require special skill for use.

Cones need slightly more practice, but they give precision control and the finest lines possible. To use, hold the cone by resting it comfortably between your thumb, palm, and first finger, and slowly squeeze it with the palm of your hand and fingers to establish an even line of paste. You may find it easier to support the cone with your other hand and/or rest the weight of your "drawing" hand on the little finger, which will help maintain a steady line. It is best to avoid holding the cone too near the tip, as this can make it hard to control and will block the flow of paste, possibly

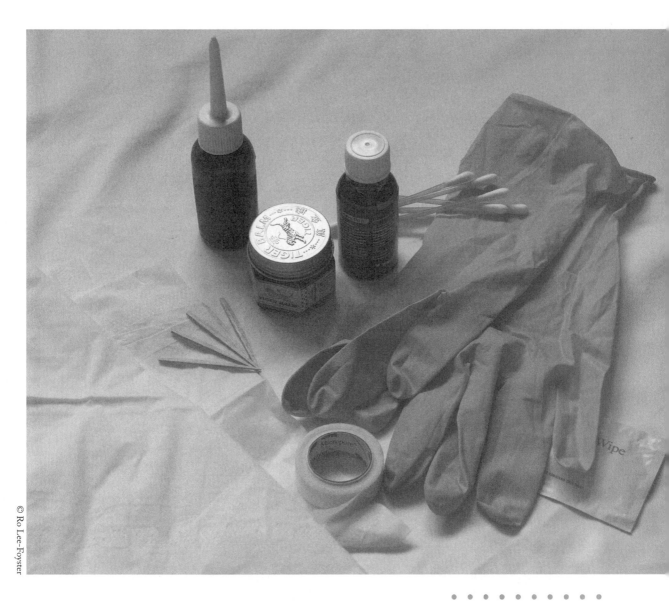

Equipment needed for
henna application

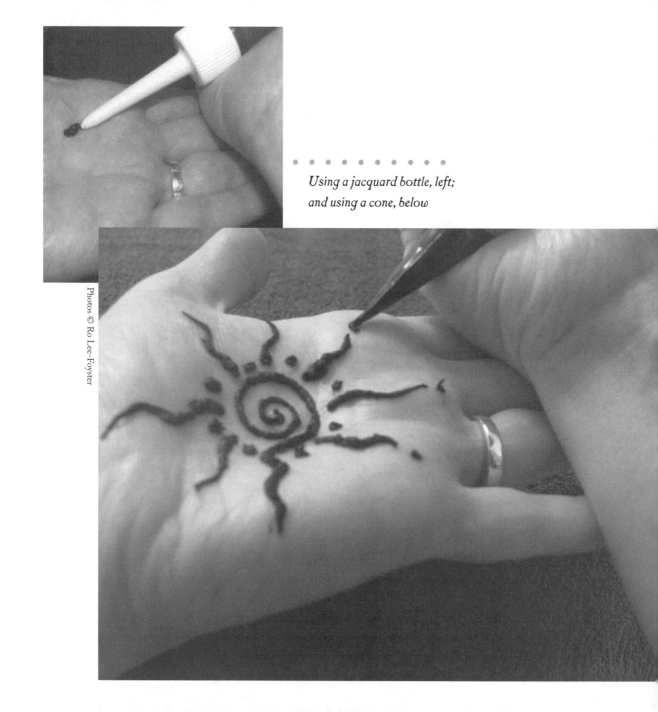

Using a jacquard bottle, left;
and using a cone, below

causing the other end to explode! As the cone empties, hold it gently by the end and roll the elastic band carefully downwards towards the tip—this will allow for a continual flow of paste as you work.

Whichever method you use to apply the henna, it is advisable to start with simple designs and practice, practice, practice. If you don't feel confident about applying the henna directly on your skin, practice on some paper first or on an area of your body that is not immediately visible. You can also use an eye pencil, a stencil, or transfer paper if you want to ease into using the henna or would like a guiding outline. Drawing your design on paper first is also a great way to get into the creative flow—try making a scrapbook of your designs and keep them for future use or for tracing onto transfer paper.

Using an Eye Pencil

This is a really good way of marking out your design before applying the henna. Use a brown eyeliner or eyebrow pencil to sketch out your pattern; you'll find it is easy to rub off if you get a wonky line.

Using Stencils

Stencils are easy to find in Middle Eastern or Indian shops and are simple to use. They are usually made from a flexible rubber material and are faintly tacky so that they can stick to the skin. The best way to use them, once you have positioned it on the skin, is to slap henna paste all over the stencil, leave it to dry, and peel it off. They probably won't give such an intricate design, but for beginners, they are fun to use.

Using Transfer Paper

Transfer paper is really useful if you want to attempt complex patterns or are just not confident about trying freehand application. You can either trace a pattern you like or print one from the computer and then copy it onto the transfer paper. Using a deodorant stick, "glue" the inked side of the transfer paper onto your skin and smooth it down. The ink then transfers the pattern to your skin, and you should have a ready-made outline to apply your henna to.[16]

· ·

Applying the Henna

Hold the cone or bottle between your thumb and first finger as if holding a pen and touch the tip of the nib/cone to the skin, using it to draw an outline of your design; you can then fill in the details one bit at a time. It may take awhile to get used to the flow of the henna, so just keep practicing. There are various henna tutorials on the Internet site YouTube that are useful to watch so that you can see the actual henna application process in real time.

Preserving Your Work

After you have created your design, you will need to fix it using the lemon juice and sugar glaze. Dab the mixture onto the touch-dried henna design with a cotton ball. This can be repeated several times, allowing the glaze to dry in between. The glaze not only helps to bring out the colour (via the lemon juice) but keeps the henna flexible (sugar), so it should not crack or flake off during the staining process.

---

16 You can buy transfer paper from Mehandi.com (see appendix) or eBay.

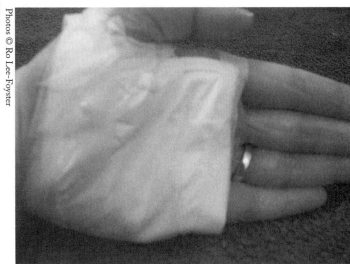

• • • • • • • • • •

*Applying fixative and
covering the design*

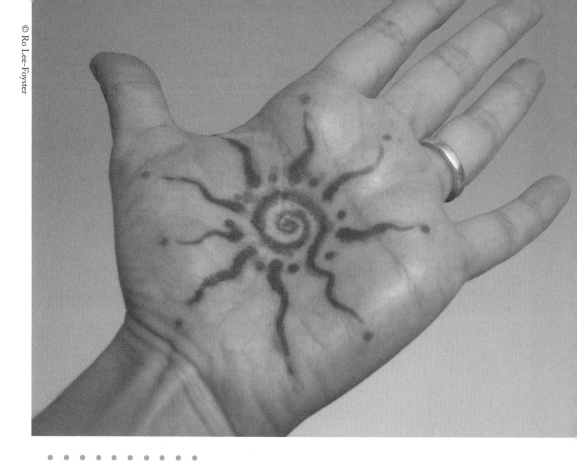

The finished design!

When you have finished applying the glaze, let the design dry naturally or use gentle direct warmth, then cover your dried design. There are a few ways you can do this. One way is to secure layers of toilet paper or tissues over the henna using surgical tape; another is to put a layer of gauze or just a layer of tape over the design. Whichever method you use, it is important to fix it securely and to keep the design warm and dry for at least eight hours. Of course, you can cover it with clothing, a glove, or a sock, depending on where you have been hennaed. You can even apply a hot water bottle or heating pad to the area to encourage the depth of colour.

When you unwrap the design, make sure you don't flake bits of henna all over an area that may stain. Carefully unpeel the tape and remove all tissue or gauze, and then gently scrape off the dried henna using your fingernail, a blunt blade, or a dry piece of towel; do not use water. You should now have a lovely henna design ranging from orange to red to reddish brown.

After you have removed the henna, try not to get it wet for at least twelve hours. The colour will keep developing for up to forty-eight hours after removal of the paste and will reach its peak, after which it will gradually lighten but last anywhere from two to four weeks. Although the henna penetrates several layers, the skin continuously regenerates and so the design will gradually fade, so it is useful to rub a little body oil or lotion regularly over the area, as this will not only protect it from moisture but will keep the skin supple and less likely to shed as quickly.

Do not despair if your design is not exactly as you would wish it to be; keep experimenting and practicing, and you will soon be a henna pro. Should you wish to know more about becoming a professional henna artist, please refer to "The Henna Page" entry in the appendix.

Removing Henna Stains

As henna stains so quickly, it is often difficult to remove it from the skin in the first day or so. However, there are ways to accelerate the fading process. If it is a tiny dot, you can probably scrub it off immediately with only a little residual stain. However, if your design goes horribly wrong and you wish to remove it, wipe the henna off as quickly as possible if it is still wet. If the design has already dried, then gently rub olive oil and/or an exfoliant (such as sea salt, sugar, or any face scrub) into the skin, which can help remove any dead skin cells. If you do not have overly sensitive skin, soak a cotton bud or swab in a hydrogen peroxide solution and rub over the stain. These may not remove the dye completely, but they should speed up the fading process.

Chapter 8

Henna Spells

Let me henna a heart on your hand; clench it,
and know that my love is within you.
—Anonymous

Magic has been a part of our universal culture for as long as there are documented records, and in one form or another, civilizations and tribal people have expressed their devotion to deities and Spirit through symbols. A symbol is like a key—it unlocks the door to the unconscious mind and conveys something that words cannot express, yet conversely is often understood the world over. Whether simple and to the point or delightfully intricate, these mystical symbols are thought to imbue us with the power behind the image, the sympathetic magic of the Divine itself.

Over the millennia, symbols became spells, mixing imagery with corresponding elements such as the planets, the zodiac, and related plants, oils, and minerals. Traditions spread and became intertwined, morphing religions and spiritual paths so that unique symbols became universal and more widely recognized. Magic itself is the art of change, and by using the elements, we can harness the invisible forces that surround us to make changes both subtle and powerful to ourselves and our environment. The use of plants and their byproducts of oils, resins, and gums have been used in magical and medicinal practices from time immemorial. Henna is

an integral part of that history and one that has been embraced worldwide. Its strangely mystical nature and indelible stain adds to its allure; what better medium to use when making magic?

The following spells and charms can be as simple or as intricate as you wish; they are open to interpretation and easy to embellish. In chapter 7, you learned how to mix and apply henna to the skin. Now you can use this skill to add some magic and mystery to your life by using several different principles:

A Symbol: To convey the intention of your spell.

Essential Oils and Herbs: To stimulate the mind and spirit, and to add magical correspondences that strengthen your intent.

Planetary and Elemental Correspondences: To enhance the power of the herbs, oils, and symbols.

By applying the appropriate henna design with intent, mixed with corresponding oils, herbs, or powders, you are creating a potent spell. As the design is temporary, you can reapply it as needed or allow it to fade as the magic does its work.

· ·
Creating Your Designs

When creating your designs, let your imagination run riot or stick to traditional symbols—whichever you feel most able to do. To start with, it may be easier to stick to simple designs until you are confident you can apply the henna easily. There are many symbols that are very striking and powerful but only use a few lines or circles, which you can embellish as you wish.

For example:

- A cross within a circle
- Add some dots around the circle and the arms of the cross
- Maybe some arrows on the arms of the cross for protection
- A heart
- Add spirals, dots, or an eye in the middle
- Add a name

If you wish to add your name or someone else's into your design, you can change it into a sigil by using the letters to overlap and create a shape, or you can use a flowing italic script and hide the name within flourishes, flowers, or shapes.

Examples of meaningful symbols
for your henna designs

The Spells

Always remember when doing any form of magic that the intent should be to do others and yourself no harm. View the force of the universe as a neutral but powerful element. We can choose what we want to do with it, so make that choice wisely.

- Beauty, 199
- Happiness, 200
- Health & Healing, 201
- Love, 203
- Protection, 206
- Purification, 208
- Sacred Spirituality, 209
- Wealth & Prosperity, 210

The relevant magical correspondences are listed as per each spell. They represent the following:

Planet: Associated with the action/emotion.

Day: The most conducive time for the spell to be applied.

Number: This also can be incorporated into the design—e.g., seven shapes or even a stylized number seven.

Herbs or Oils: Associated with the action/emotion.

Moon Phase: One that is most helpful for the particular spell.

Symbol: Represents the goal or desire and can be incorporated into your design (for inspiration, check out the symbols listed in chapter 4).

Oils

Mix the henna as per one of the recipes in chapter 7; when instructed to add the oils, use the appropriate oil for your chosen spell. Use high-grade essential oils or blends only; choose a single oil or a blend of up to five different oils, using the appropriate amount of drops for the amount of henna paste you are making, i.e., five to ten drops per tablespoon of paste.

Do not use essential oils or herbs or henna on very young children or if you are in the early stages of pregnancy.

Flowers, Herbs & Powders

Should you wish to use powders or crushed herbs, add these in with your henna when mixing the paste (see page 175). Choose two or three different herbs. To mix with the henna, crush the dried flowers, herbs, and spices with a mortar and pestle if they are not already powdered. You may need to add slightly more liquid to compensate for the extra powder. Depending on the ingredients, it may need sieving before adding to the henna powder.

To Prepare

Allow yourself plenty of time and make the area around you as comfortable (and stainproof) as possible, consecrating and purifying the area if necessary. Burn some incense, light some candles, brew up some tea, and you are ready to go!

A modern design
using hearts

....

Beauty

Place anywhere!

Element: Water

Planetary Correspondence: Venus

Number: 7

Day: Friday

Moon: Waxing

Beauty Spell

- 2 drops ylang-ylang or jasmine
- 1 drop rose

SUGGESTED DESIGNS

   Rose

   Heart

   Flowers

   Spirals

Happiness

Place over the heart, chest, belly, or anywhere.

Element: Fire

Planetary Correspondence: Sun

Number: 6

Day: Sunday

Moon: Waxing/Full

Happiness Spell

- 1 drop orange
- 1 drop bergaptene-free bergamot
- 1 drop lemon
- 1 drop benzoin

SUGGESTED DESIGNS

    Sun

    Flowers

    Spirals

Health & Healing

Place anywhere you need healing or strengthening—as the design fades, you can reapply for added power or let the ailment fade as the henna does.

Element: Fire

Planetary Correspondences: Sun (general healing), Mars (physical strength, healing after accident or surgery)

Numbers: 6, 5

Days: Sunday, Tuesday

Moon: Waxing

Symbols

Sun: Flaming sun or alchemical/planetary symbol

Mars: Alchemical (right-side-up triangle) or planetary symbol

Ankh: Ancient Egyptian symbol of good health and long life

Caduceus: Good health and healing

Sma: An ancient Egyptian symbol in the shape of the lungs

General Good Health Spell

- 2 drops oil or pinch dried lemon balm
- 2 drops oil or pinch dried, crushed, and ground lemon peel
- 1 drop oil or pinch dried, crushed, and ground sandalwood
- 1 drop oil or pinch dried jasmine flowers

Energy Blend

- 1 drop lemon
- 1 drop orange
- 1 drop ginger

Mental Health Spell

- 2 drops rosemary
- 1 drop cedarwood
- 2 drops lemon

Fertility & Conception Spell

- 2 drops geranium
- 1 drop rose
- 1 drop patchouli

Place design over the womb.

SUGGESTED DESIGNS

Moon

Venus Sigil

Ankh

Fish

Goat or Ram

Women's Healing Spell

- 1 drop oil or pinch ground rose petals
- 1 drop oil or pinch ground jasmine flowers
- 1 drop oil or pinch ground sandalwood

SUGGESTED DESIGNS

Ankh in a Circle

Flaming Sun

Caduceus

. . . .

Love

Love—the most often requested and used spell of all! As humans we are all looking for true love; use it wisely and without manipulation, as there is nothing more tragic than a case of unrequited or manipulated love. Use this spell to attract love to you in its most positive aspect—it may not attract a particular person, but it will attract the right one!

Apply your design to the heart/breast region or palm of hand.

Elements: Water (love), Fire (sex)

Planetary Correspondences: Venus (love), Mars (sex)

Numbers: 7 (Venus), 5 (Mars)

Days: Friday (Venus), Tuesday (Mars)

Moon: Waxing

Symbols

Heart: For all love spells

Heart with Eye Inside: To protect your love against others

Acorn: To attract love

Moon (Waxing Crescent): Drawn with points to the left

Venus (Planetary) Sigil: For feminine love

Apple: Love, friendship

Daisy: Innocence and love

Honeysuckle: Fidelity, affection, to dream of your true love

Lotus: Spiritual love and protection

Poppy: To help if bewitched in love or lust

Rose: Pure or divine love

Willow: Loss of love, to ease sorrow

Knot: To hold the love of a sweetheart

Love Attraction Spell

- 2 drops palmarosa
- 1 drop cardamom
- 1 drop ginger
- 1 drop ylang-ylang

Light-Hearted Love Spell

- Pinch dried rose petals
- Pinch dried lavender

- Pinch orris root
- 1 dried rosehip

Protective Love Spell

- 2 drops rose oil (or pinch dried rose petals)
- 2 drops black pepper oil (or pinch black peppercorns)

Recovery from Love Lost Spell

- Pinch dried lemon balm or 2 drops oil
- Pinch dried jasmine flower or 2 drops jasmine/ylang-ylang oil
- Pinch of orris root (omit if using the oils)

Sexual Attraction Blend

- 1 drop patchouli
- 1 drop ginger
- 1 drop cardamom

Erotic Ritual Blend

- 2 drops jasmine or ylang-ylang
- 1 drop rose maroc
  or
- 2 drops patchouli
- 1 drop cinnamon (NOTE: may irritate sensitive skin)

See erotic ritual directions on page 221; place design in more intimate areas such as breast, inner thigh, and above the pubic area.

SUGGESTED DESIGNS

To Attract Love: An upside-down triangle, snake, heart

To Protect Your Love: An eye inside a heart

To Give Love: A heart with a spiral

For Male/Female Energy: Venus/Mars sigil

For Female/Female or Male/Male: Venus/Venus or Mars/Mars sigil

For Joining/Marriage: Entwined hearts or circles

· ·

Protection

This is one of the most widely used spells across the world. In Morocco and some Middle Eastern countries, protection against the evil eye was and still is very important. The symbol used is traditionally an eye often made of blue glass with a white centre, which is hung over the door of a house or worn as an amulet (see coloured endpages for a photo). A protection spell can be used against anything that is potentially causing you harm or distress, be it an emotion (anger, misery, jealousy, or an addiction), a person, or a spirit.

Apply your design either over the solar plexus (upper abdomen) or on the palm of the hand.

Element: Fire

Planetary Correspondences: Saturn, Mars, Sun

Numbers: 3, 5, 6

Days: Saturday, Tuesday, Sunday

Moon: Waning

Symbols

Numbers: 3, 5, 6

Sun: A flaming or planetary symbol

Mars: An alchemical or planetary symbol

Circle: Universal symbol of protection

Cross within a Circle

Eye of Horus: Protection, especially powerful if both eyes are drawn

Pentagram: A five-pointed star

Pentacle: Pentagram within a circle

Hexagram: A six-pointed star or Star of David

Bell: Commonly used for banishing

Fish: To protect against the hatred of others toward you

Scarab Beetle: Protects against evil

Star: Wards off evil and draws forth good

Tassel: In the Middle East, used to repel evil spirits

Protection Spell

- 1 drop black pepper
- 1 drop clove
- 1 drop marjoram

Magical Protection Spell

- 2 drops frankincense
- 1 drop myrrh
- 2 drops sandalwood

Banishing/Hex-Breaking Spell

- 1 drop oil or pinch dried vetivert
- 1 drop oil or pinch dried juniper berries
- 1 drop oil or pinch dried basil

SUGGESTED DESIGNS

Pentacle

Flaming Sun

Eye of Horus

Cross in Circle

· ·

Purification

Place over the heart for spiritual purification, over the belly for health purification, and on the lower abdomen or pubis for cleansing after a period and to balance the menstrual cycle.

Element: Water

Planetary Correspondence: Saturn

Number: 3

Day: Saturday

Moon: Waning

Purification Blend

- 1 drop lemon
- 1 drop lime

- 1 drop grapefruit
- 1 drop orange

SUGGESTED DESIGNS

Sword with Flames

Sun or Flaming Sun

Cross in a Circle

Water Symbol

Lotus

. . . .

Sacred Spirituality

Place on the heart and hands. Use any designs that symbolize your personal spiritual path.

- 1 drop frankincense
- 1 drop sandalwood
- 1 drop myrrh
- 1 drop cedar

SUGGESTED DESIGNS

Ankh

Pentagram

Pentagon

Cross

Spiral

Dot within Circle

Wealth & Prosperity

Place your design on the palm of the hands or on the chest to receive wealth of all kinds!

Element: Earth

Planetary Correspondence: Jupiter

Number: 4

Day: Thursday

Moon: Waxing

Symbols

Four-Leaf Clover: The leaves going clockwise from left stem represent fame, wealth, love, and health, respectively

Alchemical or Planetary Sign of Jupiter

Cat

Narcissus

Nine-Pointed Star

Owl

Scarab

Sun: Planetary or alchemical symbol

Wishbone

Money Spell

- 1 drop ginger
- 1 drop vetivert
- 1 drop patchouli
- 1 drop clove

Business Success Spell

- 1 pinch dried basil
- 1 pinch ground cinnamon
- 1 pinch dried ground cedarwood

Good Luck Blend

- 1 drop/pinch patchouli
- 1 drop/pinch clove
- 1 drop/pinch cinnamon
- 1 drop/pinch orange

SUGGESTED DESIGNS

Stylized Jupiter Sigil

Pentacle

Four-Leaf Clover

Chapter 9

Henna Rituals

Daughter, let your henna be happy
Let your talk be sweet
Call your mother come here
Let her see her daughter become bride
—Turkish folk song

What could be more special than to re-create a traditional ritual but attune it to your own beliefs or ideals? For an original and truly memorable experience, use any of the following rituals as a template for your own celebration or remembrance occasion. The power and beauty of henna is something that no one will forget, regardless of the circumstance—it could be for a betrothal or engagement, a wedding or handfasting, a baby shower, birth, milestone celebration, or even to mark the passing of a loved one. These very intimate yet universal rituals can be used by anyone of any faith or creed as a way of honoring the times that we often reflect back on.

. . . .

Engagement, Wedding, or Handfasting

A very special and genuine occasion whereby two people are joined in a commitment to love, cherish, and honor each other. As we have seen in previous chapters,

betrothal, wedding, or love rituals and the corresponding designs are used the world over and offer the couple and their family and friends the opportunity to do something unique and very special aside from the main event. It is a chance to have a serious yet lighthearted celebration that can be a part of the more formal wedding ceremony or as an alternative to an engagement, hen (bachelorette), or stag party.

Ideally, the henna ritual needs to be held at someone's home, as the hennee (the person being hennaed) has to be comfortable, often for long periods.

The ideal theme for such a party would be to connect it to a region that has embraced henna as a tradition, such as India, Egypt, or the Middle East. Allow your imagination to run wild and include anything that would make it seem exotic and sumptuous.

Ancient Egypt

Prepare an Egyptian feast with a long table loaded with delicacies, wine, and beer, while the pharaoh and his queen-to-be lounge on cushions, waiting to be hennaed and fed. Burn kyphi incense for good fortune and to appease the gods, and make an offering to Hathor and Horus, the two deities that were brought together in ancient Egyptian festivals to celebrate their sacred marriage.

DESIGNS TO TRY

Hearts

Symbols of Hathor and Horus

Sun and moon

Hieroglyphs of the two lovers' names

Indian Dreams

Another idea would be an Indian "Bollywood" theme, with vibrant colours, costumes, and music. Indulge in delicious Indian cuisine (finger food is best) and sumptuous fruity cocktails or smoothies. Get your guests dancing while you get hennaed—after all, you need entertaining too!

DESIGNS TO TRY

> Hearts
>
> Flowers and vines
>
> Fruits
>
> Hindu calligraphy of the two lovers' names

Turkish Delight

Create an Arabian Nights-style tent theme with cushions, rugs, and lanterns, with "servants" offering delicate sweetmeats and iced mint tea. Use scented candles in sensuous fragrances such as rose and jasmine and have rose petals strewn on the floor. Play some hauntingly beautiful Arabic music, hire a belly dancer, and throw caution to the wind with some seriously exotic celebrations. Try using a design whereby you hide your lover's name somewhere within it—and see how long it takes for them to find it!

DESIGNS TO TRY

> Hearts
>
> Flowers
>
> Geometric intertwined shapes
>
> Arabic calligraphy of the two lovers' names

*Lovely examples
of bump decor*

Pregnancy or Baby Shower

As mentioned in previous chapters, numerous countries have used the tradition of applying henna during the last stage of pregnancy. In Morocco and India, a henna pattern applied to the belly of the woman has long been a ritual used to protect and bless both mother and child. It was believed to keep them safe from any malicious or evil spirits who may have drawn close as birth approached. The passage of birth has often been deemed to be a dangerous journey for the new infant, and the strength and power of henna's sacred dye used in combination with protective designs was one way of guarding against malevolent influences, or djinn (see chapter 3). Henna was also regarded as being able to ease the process of birth and bring about a healthy child. It is certainly very relaxing having a design applied to your belly and all the pampering that ensues.

Modernly, women can incorporate this beautiful ritual into our own culture, using the power of henna to celebrate the marvel that is our ability to create and

© Maggie Johnston

sustain new life inside us. A wonderful way of sharing this process would be to have a baby shower with a difference—not only does the mother-to-be get hennaed but all her friends could have an accompanying henna design to help protect and bless the mom and baby.

As pregnancy is a very special time, it is a lovely idea to make a celebration of the last weeks, for soon the harder work will come! A henna pregnancy ritual should therefore be one of calmness and serenity, with all the guests waiting on the expectant mother as if she were a queen. You can really go to town with the preparations, maybe having a theme such as a Middle Eastern harem or a garden paradise. Make sure it is wonderfully comfortable for the mom-to-be, with plenty of cushions to prop her up and make her as comfortable as possible. Add music, candles, and exotic food for a delightfully memorable evening, and make sure someone has a camera to record the event for a special entry in the baby album. Although the design should last at least 7–10 days, it is a great time to create memories that will last a lifetime, and it is something that the mom can show her daughter or son in years to come.

Use only natural henna mixed with lemon juice and sugar for this process, although a few drops of rose or orange flower water are perfectly safe to add at this stage of the pregnancy. If the pregnant woman is very anemic or has any other medical conditions, it is best to check with a midwife or doctor first. Do make sure that the person applying the henna is aware of any concerns and that they have made a gentle mixture.

DESIGNS TO TRY

Sun: Protection, health

Eye: Protection

Spirals: Protection, spiritual awareness, and direction

Fruit: Mangoes (paisley), pomegranates, figs

Moon: Attunement with the baby through lunar/watery symbolism

Stars: To represent the divine origin of the spirit, hope, and beauty

Astrological signs: For expected month of birth

Planetary signs: To correspond with astrological signs and/or personality traits that you would like to bestow on your child

And if you know your child's gender:

Male: Mars, Jupiter, Mercury, sun

Female: Venus, moon

Fairies: A connection to the unseen realm

Baby: Allow the artist to paint your baby onto your belly as you or they visualize them

· ·

Purification Ritual

If you feel that you need a good cleansing, then this ritual is perfect for you. Use it if you are physically under the weather, if you feel you are under attack mentally or spiritually, to generally clear your personal space and the environment, or before you embark on any spiritual work. Purification rituals have been used for thousands of years (see chapter 3) and usually involve some form of ritual washing or fumigation with incense and the creation of a talisman for wearing or carrying. With henna, you can take this one step further and apply the talisman to yourself.

You will need:

- Water (set up in the bathroom or have a large bowl of clean, fresh water at hand)
- Towels
- Body cloth
- Soap or hammam scrub
- Henna paste and applicator (make up in advance—see chapter 7)
- Incense (optional)
- Flowers (optional)
- Music (optional)

Firstly, make sure you are able to concentrate on the work at hand; it is probably best to have the house or at least the bathroom to yourself, and make sure you will not be disturbed—turn off the phone and lock the door. Purification preferably needs to be done alone, or if you are following it with the erotic ritual later in this chapter, then it is fine to do it with your partner. Create a comfortable space and ensure you have towels, soap, and your henna mix ready. Put on some music, burn some incense or throw some rose petals in the bath or bowl of water, and then relax in a seated position for ten minutes.

Concentrate fully on what it is you wish to achieve through purification—better health or a detox, ridding yourself of negative influences, or just to create a pure body, mind, and spirit. Then begin to wash yourself from head to foot; use your hand, a body cloth, or salt scrub, and work in long, sweeping strokes along your arms, body, and legs. You can wash your hair if you have time and the facilities. All the time you are washing yourself, imagine that you are rinsing away negative energies, sweeping any impurities into the bath or basin with each rinse of the cloth. When you feel that you have achieved a state of cleanliness, empty the bath or bowl of water while imagining all negativity swirling down the drain.

It is a common magical practice to do a final rinse with cold water (if you can bear it) or hold your hands in a bowl or basin of cold water for a minute or two, then drain it away as before. Dry yourself thoroughly, and if you need to warm up, wrap yourself in a robe or towel.

Now you can apply your henna design on the body part you wish to decorate. For purification, the palms, soles of feet, or the belly are powerful points, and symbols should be bold or flowing to illustrate the output of energy.

DESIGNS TO TRY

Spirals

Water: Drops, waves, or watery designs

Fire or flames: For powerful purification whereby you may need to burn away stubborn negative energies

If you would like to continue with the erotic ritual, it may be wise to wait until later to henna yourself rather than spoil the wet design during intimate moments!

Erotic Ritual

After the purification ritual, you may wish to continue on to the erotic ritual along with a partner. Make sure you are somewhere warm and comfortable where you won't be disturbed—lock the doors, take the phone off the hook, and turn off the cell phone! Because you are using henna, make sure that the couch, floor, or bed has a protective sheet over it, but make it look like part of the theme. This is an opportunity for you both as lovers to spend some time really focusing on your intimate feelings and sharing some deep thoughts. Burn some appropriate incense or diffuse some sultry essential oils (rose, ylang-ylang, or jasmine); light candles, close the drapes, dim the lights, and turn on some slow, mellow music.

The intent of this ritual can be entirely up to you, but the essence is to bond with your partner in a sensual way. In Indian tantric practice, much emphasis is placed on creating a pleasurable and erotic environment before any actual sexual performance, and it is the perfect way to bring about a sense of mutual trust. The focus is on the breath and sensual contact with the intention of creating a spiritual union between you and your partner by circulating what Easterners call *chi*, or internal energy. The aim is to transcend beyond the purely physical experience of sexual activity.

Sit or stand facing each other, and look deeply into one another's eyes while you allow your breathing to follow your partner's. As you inhale, bring energy up from your heart, and as you exhale, lean in towards your partner and gently touch your foreheads together, letting your love flow into them. Contemplate for a few moments what this person means to you, and perhaps you can tell them exactly that. Spend some time gently stroking your partner's arms, back, or neck, but try not to get too distracted, for you have work to do! The aim of this ritual is more to connect with your partner emotionally and spiritually than physically. When you are relaxed and feeling at one with your partner, ask them if you can now apply your chosen henna design on their body. This can be a prearranged symbol or design, or it may be something that you wish to experiment with as the moment takes you. It is a good idea to place the design in an intimate or hidden area of the body, as this is something that only you two will share. The breast, inner thigh, lower back, or the belly are perfect areas to choose. Apply the henna with intent—for love, devotion, or lust, or to honor your lover. This should be a sensual and deeply connecting experience; make sure your partner is comfortable, warm, and feeling totally loved. If they feel confident enough, allow them to return the compliment and apply a design on your body—this can be the same as the one you gave them or it could be totally different; the choice is yours as a couple.

DESIGNS TO TRY

Hearts intertwined

Magical symbols relating to you and your partner: e.g.,
Mars (masculine), Venus (feminine)

Vines

Spirals

You will then need to cover the drying henna to preserve your design; see chapter 7 for instructions.

• •

Celebration Henna Ritual
For Good Luck, Leaving Home,
Coming Home, Birthdays, or Anniversaries

Considering its connection with good fortune, protection, and celebration, you can use a henna theme for any party. The list is almost as large as your imagination, and it would make a very original occasion for anything from a teen birthday to a charity fundraiser. You could hire a henna artist or just experiment on each other. Teens love the chance to mix old and new designs to create their very own "temporary tattoos."

As a fundraising idea, you could hold a henna harem; ask for a donation for every design applied, and offer special "mehndi" cakes and cookies for sale.

Making a Magical Mehndi Cake

For very special occasions, you could make an intricate magical mehndi cake that does not actually have henna in it but is made to look as if it has been hennaed. By creating a magical design on the cake with coloured frosting, it can become an

*A collection of teen
hennaed hands, above;
a magical mehndi cake, right*

edible talisman! Made with love and intention, each piece that is eaten is imbued with the energy and power connected with the iced design. This method is a very ancient one and has been used by magicians the world over to ingest magical energy via their food and drink; by focusing on the desired intent while preparing the food and beverages, the magician can put the required force into it, and every cell can then benefit from the resulting "charge."

It is a wonderful way of creating health-giving food for yourself and others. Think of all the different festival foods we eat that date back from very old traditions or religions—at Easter, we have hot cross buns (the cross can represent the goddess Eostre, the four quarters, or the cross of crucifixion) and simnel cake (the eleven marzipan balls used to decorate the top represent eleven disciples). The matzo of Passover and *sol et lune* bread are reputed to have evolved from alchemy with their allusion to the sun and moon.

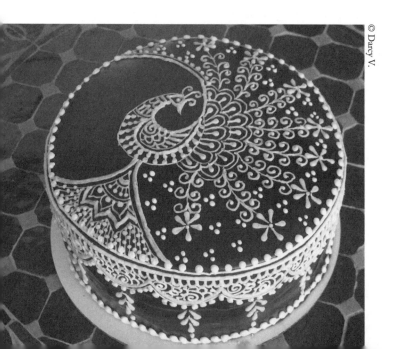

© Darcy V.

How to Mehndi Your Cake

Make a sponge or fruit cake using your favourite recipe or store-bought mix, or buy a ready-made cake from a store. You will then need to ice it (if not already iced) to create a base for your mehndi-style design.

For the frosting, you will need:

- 1 egg white
- 2 cups or 250 grams sifted powdered frosting sugar

Start with the egg white in a bowl and gradually add the frosting sugar in small amounts, stirring all the time. Continue beating until it becomes firm and shiny and little peaks appear when you lift out the spoon. Now you have a choice—you need to have one colour to coat the surface of the cake and one for the actual mehndi design. Divide your frosting into two bowls and add food colouring as required to the paste; re-create the appearance of henna by carefully adding drops of your chosen colour(s) until you achieve the desired shade, which can range anywhere from orange to reddish brown to brownish black. You could even use melted chocolate if you are feeling decadent, or choose ready-made tubes of frosting or edible icing pens if you are feeling unconfident or pushed for time.

Leave the frosting to stand for a few minutes before using, and then pour onto the surface of the cake. The frosting will spread out slowly; use a spatula to even out the mixture until you get a perfect layer. To make the mehndi patterns, pour the frosting into a cone (just like the one used to apply henna onto the skin) or a piping bag, and decorate your cake with your chosen design.

DESIGNS TO TRY

Sun: For health and energy

Sun and moon: For balance, male and female, weddings (sacred marriage)

Magical symbols: Planetary or alchemical

Zodiac signs: For birthdays

Two hennaed hands: For weddings/handfasting

Calligraphy: For naming ceremonies or births

Hearts: For weddings/handfasting, Valentine's Day, or love rituals

Khamsa and hamsa hands: For protection (e.g., travel or leaving home)

Other Fun Things to Do for Henna Parties

Make cards to use as invites to your henna celebrations by tracing a hand and decorating it using pens, paints, or even henna! Why not henna your palm and print it onto the card? Some henna artists will henna anything—canvasses, lampshades, plates, candles, jewelry boxes—so let your imagination run riot and have fun with the henna, making magical designs for your home.

If you have children at the festivities, keep them occupied while the moms get hennaed by getting them to design henna "handprints." Cut some hand shapes out of paper or card stock in advance, and get the kids to draw patterns on the templates with crayons, pens, or paint. They can then keep the "hands" as a good luck charm to stick on their wall.

Make henna cakes or cookies—have some ready-made cupcakes or hand/foot-shaped cookies (you can buy hand- or foot-shaped cookie cutters online), and get the children to mehndi the cakes with chocolate frosting. Yummy!

Passing Ritual:
For the Deceased, the Living, and the Grieving

This is a difficult and often taboo subject to deal with, but it's one that dominates our lives, for at some point we will all lose a loved one; indeed, we will all die. In many cultures throughout the ages, death has been dealt with in different ways, with rituals, ceremonies, and blessings. The common factor is that any ceremony fulfills the needs not only of the deceased but of those left behind. On all levels—be they mental, physical, or spiritual—our species has always needed a way of dealing with the passing of life. The ancient Egyptians were strong believers in the premise of an afterlife and did everything they could to ensure a place amongst the gods. The process of mummification took up to seventy days and was accompanied by rituals, adornment of the body, and a multitude of prayers and offerings. Nowadays, we do not have the time or the resources to emulate this wonderful practice, but we can still do many things to honor our dead and send them on their way with dignity and respect.

Loss, grief, anger, sorrow, and loneliness are just a few of the emotions that can overwhelm us when a close friend or family member dies. The act of acknowledging this is vitally important and is something that is prevalent the world over in the form of a funeral. But we should not overlook the needs of the dying or deceased one; their spiritual well-being is something that many of us think of but are perhaps unsure of how to go about preserving. In almost all cultures, a ritual washing and dressing of the dead is commonplace; perhaps embalming takes place, and then a funeral of varying types. However, in the Western world we are less likely to view this as preparation for a journey into the afterlife and more as being a respectful thing to do. In Africa and India, rituals are more steeped in spiritual meaning and prepare the deceased for the next leg of their eternal journey; often the dead are decorated with henna and finely dressed as if for their wedding day. For those of us in the West who are more spiritually inclined, the lack of participation in our loved one's path to the afterlife can be quite harrowing. The sterile confines of a hospital, the slightly better environment of the hospice, or the comfort and safety of home are the options we have if we have time to plan the remaining days. Often we do not have the choice, and so it is difficult to know what to do when faced with the inevitable. Even though to others it may seem morbid, it may be useful to talk to your family about what you would like to happen when you are dying or have died, or if your family would like something special for themselves. In the bustle of modern healthcare and under the difficult circumstances following a death, it may be almost impossible to do what we would like, but it is important that the wishes of the dying and their relatives and friends are taken into consideration. If necessary, it can be made a legal requirement that your and their wishes are carried out.

There are several ways that we can make a difference for both the living and the dead; following are two rituals that can be used before and after death.

Anointing the Dying:
The Henna Ritual of Peace

It is possible that many of our loved ones, friends, and even ourselves will succumb to a protracted or terminal illness that would involve care during our last days either within a hospice or, if we are lucky enough, in our own home. These days can be made much more pleasant if we can have time to reflect, reconcile, and gently celebrate the life of the dying one. It will not be easy, but it can be done with dignity and great love.[17]

---

17 An amazing book that covers some of these issues is *Intimate Death: How the Dying Teach Us to Live* by Marie de Hennezel.

If possible, spiritually clear the room where the ill person is lying by lighting some incense, sprinkling salt water, or placing candles in the four corners. Decorate the room with flowers, candles (if health and safety permit it), and any personal mementoes such as photos, letters, trinkets, and treasures. Play some music, sing, and spritz or diffuse some essential oils for fragrance into the air; this has often been a comfort to the dying and a requisite of death. The area needs to be imbued with the spirit of the dying person to create a strong and personal resonance. Have some henna already mixed up with essential oils of lavender, rose maroc, or jasmine added.

If the dying person is conscious, ask them if they have a favorite symbol; if not, agree on a suitable design that everyone in the room is willing to share. The henna can be applied to any part of the body, but the palm of the hand or just over the heart is especially potent. Gently apply a simple design on the loved one, all the while allowing your love and gratitude for their life to flow into the symbol; remember that this is something that they will take with them. While you are hennaing the other members of the family and friends, one by one they can go and tell their loved one how much they love them and anything else that needs to be said. Tears may well flow, but so will the love and respect that your loved one can then take with them on their journey.

DESIGNS TO TRY

Heart

A favorite flower

The name of a special person

A spiral or circle: To represent eternity and immortality

A religious symbol of their faith

Anubis: The guardian of the underworld

Anointing the Dead:
The Henna Ritual of Transition

This is fine if the loved one has died at home, but it may not be easy if the person has died in hospital, although it is well worth asking if the staff would allow an hour or so of quiet time for the family and friends to spend with the deceased. If there is a chapel of rest, then it certainly may be possible. Many care homes ask dying people and their families to fill out a care plan, which will include any religious or personal requests; they will then allow you to lay out the deceased should you wish to do so.

In some traditions, the soul of a person is believed to remain with the body for three days after death; this is a time of transition for the departed, and performing a ritual can be useful for helping the spirit to find its way.

If the deceased has not been laid out, prepare the area by lighting some incense and candles. Fill a bowl with scented water (maybe rose or orange flower water), and, using a clean linen cloth, wash the body quietly, gently, and with deep reverence. Remember the person as they were in life and let love and respect flow from you to them in their silent and still state. Gently comb their hair, and cover them with a white cotton or linen sheet.

If you are able, invite friends and family into the room and ask them to light a candle or leave a small offering that is pertinent to the person. Have some pre-mixed henna at hand to which oils of frankincense, myrrh, and cedar have been added. If you have not had a chance to discuss the appropriate design beforehand, decide on a symbol that you would like to use—one that represents the deceased or one for protection or fortune in the afterlife. Gently apply the design to the heart or palm of the hand while everyone focuses on the spirit of the loved one, sending waves of courage, love, and blessings. When you have finished, you may also anoint the body with oils or more henna on the forehead, the heart, and the

feet. Each person remaining can then have their palm or heart hennaed while incense is burned, music played quietly, or people pray, sing, or chant. The symbol is to create an everlasting bond between you and the deceased, and it also is a way of allowing the initial pain of grief to gently disperse as the henna stain fades gradually from your skin.

DESIGNS TO TRY

Heart

Flower

Spiral

Cross

Circle(s)

Anubis: The guardian of the underworld

Magical Henna Journal

A beautiful way to make a note of your henna rituals and designs is to create a magical henna journal. You can use your creative flair to embellish an ordinary notebook or journal, or buy a specially made one (see Maison Kenzi's henna sketchbook in the appendix). It is possible to henna cardboard or stiff paper with excellent results, and once varnished this would make a superb cover for your journal. Use it to record your designs, add photographs, make up your own rituals and recipes, and jot down your dreams and aspirations. It would also make a stunning present for a friend or loved one.

Make the magic of henna part of your life, and you will find that it attracts the power and essence of the ancient world to bestow the timeless gift of modern mystical beauty.

Bibliography

Abu Dawud Hadiths, Book 33, Hadith #4154 Agreed Upon by Nasai, http://www.searchtruth.com.

Agrippa von Nettesheim, Heinrich Cornelius. *The Three Books of Occult Philosophy, A Complete Edition*. U.S.: Llewellyn Publications, 1993.

Ali, Abdullah Yusuf, and Kitab Bhavan. *The Holy Qu'ran: English Translation, Commentary and Notes with Full Arabic Text*. New Delhi: Kitab Bhavan, 2001.

American Standard Version Bible, http://onlineparallelbible.com.

Cartwright-Jones, Catherine. "Henna in the Ancient Egyptian Pharmacopoeia: The Ebers Papyrus," http://www.hennapage.com /henna/encyclopedia/medical/ebers.html.

———. "The Functions of Childbirth and Postpartum Henna Traditions," http://www.hennapage.com/henna/what/freebooks /HPJpp2.pdf.

———. "Henna and War," http://www.hennapage.com/henna /encyclopedia/war/talons.html.

———. "Menstruation and Henna: Pollution and Purification: Henna's role in Muslim Traditions Regarding Reproductive Blood," http: //www.hennapage.com/henna/encyclopedia/HennaMenstruation.pdf.

———. "Henna and Horses: Springtime Festivals in Lebanon," http://www.hennapage.com/henna/encyclopedia/horses/springfest.html.

Ceram, C. W. *The March of Archeology.* New York: Knopf, 1958.

Coelho, Paolo. *The Pilgrimage: A Contemporary Quest for Ancient Wisdom.* London: Thorsons, 1999.

Crowley, Aleister. *Liber O [vel Manus et Sagittae sub Figura VI], Equinox Vol.1: 2.* London: Simpkin, Marshall, Hamilton, Kent & Co., Ltd., 1909.

Cunningham, Scott. *The Complete Book of Incense, Oils and Brews.* U.S.: Llewellyn Publications, 1989.

———. *Cunningham's Encyclopedia of Magical Herbs.* U.S.: Llewellyn Publications, 1985.

Epstein, Rabbi Dr. I. *Soncino Babylonian Talmud, Translated into English with Notes, Glossary and Indices.* London, Soncino Press, 1935.

de Hennezel, Marie. *Intimate Death: How the Dying Teach Us to Live.* Little, Brown & Co., 1997.

mathildasanthropologyblog.wordpress.com/2008/07/21/mummies-and-mummy-hair-from-ancient-egypt/

Husang, Alam. "Henna" (Vol.12), Encyclopaedia Iranica Online, 2004.

"Jewish Henna Ceremony." http://www.jewishtreats.org/2009/05/henna.html.

Khan, Dr. M. Laiq Ahmed. "Henna (Mehndi) is a Great Healer." http://www.islamicvoice.com/november.99/tibb.htm.

King James Bible, http://www.kingjamesbibleonline.org/

Manniche, Lise. *An Ancient Egyptian Herbal.* London: British Museum
  Publications Ltd., 1989.

Morrison, Dorothy. *Everyday Magic: Spells and Rituals for Modern
  Living.* U.S.: Llewellyn Publications, 1998.

Naidu, Sarojini. "The Golden Threshold." Project Gutenberg,
  http://www.gutenberg.org/ebooks/680.

Rider Haggard, Henry. "Smith and the Pharaohs, and Other Tales."
  http://www.gutenberg.org/etext/6073.

"Searching for the Henna Djinn." http://www.hennadervish.com
  /ddjinn02.html.

Appendix
Henna Resources & Information

. . . .

Contacts and Suppliers

All henna artists and suppliers in this section are known to the author and offer the highest quality service and supplies.

As there are only a limited amount of artists and suppliers I can mention, a comprehensive list of quality certified members may be found on the ICNHA (International Certification for Natural Henna Arts) website at www.icnha.org.

. . . .
UK

Henna Boy

Worldwide suppliers in henna powder, indigo powder, amla, *Cassia obovata,* and natural hair dyes and conditioners. Supplies premixed henna paste for immediate use.

See also entry under *Henna Artists*
www.henna-boy.co.uk

Henna Pens

Henna Penna, the pen filled with henna extract for producing easy henna designs on any part of the body that dry quickly and last for up to ten days. Henna

Penna only contains 100 percent natural ingredients—no PPD, preservatives, synthetic colourants, or perfumes, and it is not tested on animals.

www.hennapens.com

Essential Oils

NHR Organic Essential Oils

Certified organic essential oils and flower waters.

> NHR Organic Oils
> 24 Chatham Place
> Brighton
> BN1 3TN
> United Kingdom

or

> NHR Organic Oils
> Dept. AA566
> P.O. Box 618001
> Dallas, TX 75261-8001

Tel 0845-310-8066 (UK local call rate) or 1-866-816-0195 (USA toll free) or +44 1273 746 505 (International)

info@nhrorganicoils.com

USA

Mehandi: Hair, Body Care, and Body-Art Supplies

Probably the most comprehensive site, offering everything and more that you could ever want to beautify yourself naturally. Mehandi.com are suppliers of the highest quality body-art henna (including premixed paste), accessories for henna application, e-books, soaps, skincare, perfume, and even shampoo for your pets.

Associated with the Henna Page, the site also offers the Henna School, the ultimate kit that includes everything you need to become a henna artist.

Shop located at 135 E. Main St. in Kent, Ohio.

Phone: 330–238-4097 or 330-673-0600

info@mehandi.com

www.mehandi.com

Maison Kenzi: Online Henna Shop

Suppliers of finest quality henna body-art kits (starter to professional), henna powder, stencils, gloves, essential oils, and Kenzi's unique henna sketchbook full of templates to spark your creative process. The site also offers step-by-step instructions on the application of henna and many examples of henna designs.

See also entry under *Henna Artists.*

www.kenzi.com

Henna Caravan: All the Supplies for Your Henna Journey

Henna Caravan is dedicated to providing high quality henna body-art kits and supplies and has a large range of henna powders, paste, accessories, pattern books, and natural body care. Shipping is worldwide; samples and wholesale quantities available.

info@HennaCaravan.com

www.hennacaravan.com

· · · · · · ·

Canada

Henna Sooq

Your one-stop shop for professional henna (mehndi) services and supplies— high quality henna kits, powder, premixed paste, accessories, essential oils, henna

design books, stencils, natural skin and hair care. Henna Sooq also offers monthly free samples and is able to supply wholesale quantities.

See also entry under *Henna Artists.*

www.hennasooq.com

. . . .
Australia

Henna Moon

The first shop in Australia to specialize in all aspects of natural henna services and products, situated in Fremantle, Western Australia. Henna Moon online offers a great range of henna kits, powders, pastes, accessories, and applicators, alongside natural skin and hair care.

P.O. Box 1655
Fremantle, Western Australia 6959
Phone: (08) 9949-4669
Mobile: 0407-633-386
info@hennamoon.com.au
www.hennamoon.com.au

Henna Oasis

Henna Oasis is located on the Northern Gold Coast and supplies professional-grade paste, mini kits, and a beginner's guide to henna. Artists are available for hen's nights, parties, weddings, and other functions.

Phone: 0412-245-749
info@hennaoasis.com.au
www.hennaoasis.com.au

Henna Artists

UK

Glasgow

Farah Khan

Henna artist and author of *The First British Book of Henna Art*. Farah offers a mobile bridal henna service in and around the Glasgow area, party henna for friends and family, charity henna stalls, carnivals, fairs, and council workshops. She also teaches henna art privately—no experience necessary and no age limit. Henna tutorials and a portfolio are available for viewing on YouTube under "Learn Henna Art" by Farah Khan.

Phone: 07854-370-343
Contact Salon: Roshini, Maxwell Road, Glasgow, G41
mrsasid@hotmail.com
http://www.farahkhan.vpweb.co.uk/default.html

London and Sheffield

Sarah Ali Khan, HennaPro Henna

HennaPro offers henna for weddings, parties, and just for fun. The professional classes teach all aspects of henna application and design, including how to decorate items for the home with henna!

Phone: 07864-094-141
info@hennapro.com
www.hennapro.com

Kiran Sahib, Love Mehndi

Kiran Sahib is a self-taught London-based artist who specializes in traditional and modern henna art. She is principal artist at Love Mehndi and has been wowing everyone with her artistic flair and her striking Eastern and Arabian designs.

Phone: 01708-784602
Mobile: 07940-133669
kiran_sahib@hotmail.com
www.lovemehndi.co.uk

Samara Farook, Henna & Makeup Artist

Samara is a freelance henna and makeup artist specializing in all types of makeup: bridal, registry, and photographic and media makeup. Free consultations.

Services include bridal makeup and hair, including dupatta pinning and jewelry setting; beauty/fashion shoots; portfolio shoots with professional photographer; catwalk/TV/editorial.

Phone: 07737646955
info@devinebeauty.co.uk
http://www.facebook.com/l/efe89;www.devinebeauty.co.uk

Leeds

Amrit Bansal, Henna Artist

Amrit offers henna on the body for all occasions and is happy to travel to customers. She also decorates mirrors, photo frames, and jewelry boxes with henna.

Phone: 07843172336
amrit1989@hotmail.co.uk
http://www.facebook.com/pages/henna-mendhi-body-design/79578587395?ref=mf

Slough, Berkshire

Riffat—Mehndi Magic, Henna & Makeup

Riffat has over twenty-five years of experience in mehndi and offers a free consultation and the chance to be beautifully made up in the comfort of your home/venue, and is available for weddings, parties, makeovers, corporate and charity events.

Phone: 01753 554 557
Mob: 07944 341 563
info@riffat.co.uk
www.riffat.co.uk/

Brighton

Henna Boy Studio & Supplies

Henna artists and suppliers of body-art quality henna and accessories. Worldwide suppliers in henna powder, indigo powder, amla, *Cassia obovata*, and natural hair dyes and conditioners.

Henna Boy is available for bookings for corporate events, parties, weddings, charity functions, girl nights in, and any other event that you can possibly think of!

Previous clients include Brighton Pier, Microsoft, Virgin Radio, Bradford College, Glastonbury Festival, Strawberry Fair, Gay Pride Brighton, Party in the Park Brighton, Fatboy Slim Beach Party, Womad Festival, Guildford Festival, Warm Rain, Tesco, and many more...

Hendra Holiday Park Lane
Newquay, Cornwall TR8 4NY
Phone: 01637-851313
www.henna-boy.co.uk

USA

New York

Henna by Kenzi—Modern Mystical Adornment

Kenzi traces her passion for henna to the time she spent living and working in Morocco. A self-taught professional henna artist, her experience is as vast as her influences. Her work has been featured in movies (Spike Lee's *The 25th Hour* and Jonathan Demme's *The Manchurian Candidate*) and on MTV (Erykah Badu's video for "Love of My Life"), and she has also created original pieces for photo shoots and fashion shows. Kenzi also works at large-scale corporate events and festivals (such as Bulgari, HBO, and Le Tigre), as well as intimate weddings, parties, and private consultations. She also teaches the art of henna in workshops around New York City.

www.kenzi.com

San Francisco

Henna Lounge

Darcy V. is a henna artist, visual artist, and body-art supplier based in the San Francisco area.

Phone: (415) 215-6901

info@hennalounge.com

www.hennalounge.com

Canada

Winnipeg, Manitoba

Kim Brennan, Henna Artist

All events catered for—birthdays, weddings, Sangeet and bridal parties, corporate events or personal appointments.

Phone: 1 (204) 775-2786

baqnblaq69@hotmail.com

www.winnipeghenna.com

Toronto, Ontario

Henna Sooq—Henna/mehndi artist, Khadija Dawn Carryl

Henna Sooq's artists are available for your special occasion: Eid, weddings (bridal and guests), get-togethers, fundraisers, private sessions, and more. They also hold workshops.

For information on services, and to book your event:

Phone: (905) 230-4651

info@hennasooq.com

www.hennasooq.com

London, Ontario

Margaret Johnston—Mehandi by Maggie

All-natural henna body art in London, Ontario, and surrounding area (inclusive of GTA).

Phone: 519-453-0653

sari_girl@rogers.com

Montreal, Quebec

Henna Sooq

See previous entry on page 241.
Contact: Qudsiya Rauf
qudsiya@hennasooq.com

Australia

Henna Moon

Henna Moon offers supplies and natural henna body-art services in the Fremantle and Perth areas of Western Australia. An extensive range of designs are available, with something to suit every taste. Artwork is applied freehand by experienced henna artists, providing an authentic experience into the world of natural henna art.

See previous entry on page 242 for contact information.

Henna Oasis

Henna artists specializing in traditional body art. Henna Oasis is located on the Northern Gold Coast and is available to travel throughout Brisbane and the Gold Coast.

Contact: Elizabeth Prince, henna artist
See previous entry on page 242 for contact information.

Henna Resources & Information

The Henna Page

The Henna Page is an educational resource devoted to the history, traditions, techniques, science, and art of henna, and is part of a site group devoted to henna and related arts.

Catherine Cartwright-Jones' superb resource site offers everything you need to know about henna. Catherine is the world's foremost authority on all aspects of henna, including its history and chemical make-up. The website is extensive, with an enormous "Hennapedia," a forum, tutorials, free henna patterns/calendar/images, in-depth information about the dangers of black henna, and a comprehensive link section. Click through from the site to visit mehandi.com, suppliers of everything henna (see page 240).

For full details on the dangers of black henna, see http://www.hennapage.com/henna/ppd/index.html.

www.hennapage.com

Spellstone—Alex Morgan

Alex Morgan is a UK-based artist/illustrator, designer, and photographer. Her astounding work involves many books of henna patterns such as Warrior, Tribal Part I & II, and Origins Part I & II, which have also influenced her creative flair in the designs she produced for Luna Guitars. Spellstone also offers a range of design and illustration services, including custom-created graphics and logos. See Alex's work at:

www.spellstone.com
www.tapdancinglizard.com
www.lunaguitars.com

Henna Caravan

An excellent site that offers in-depth tutorials on all aspects of henna application and aftercare. It also has a henna forum and online shop.

www.hennacaravan.com

Henna Craft

Henna Craft is Humna Mustafa's website that showcases her extraordinary talent as an artist working with henna, not only on the body but on canvas, paper, and other media. A fascinating look at what can be achieved with inspiration and henna!

See Humna's work at:

www.hennacraft.com.au

www.diyastudio.com

Henna Tribe

An online community, informational resource, and professional network for anyone interested in the ancient art of applying henna to skin.

http://hennatribe.org/

Recommended Reading

Any of the henna and body-art e-books from TapDancing Lizard Publications: Includes titles by Catherine Cartwright-Jones, Alex Morgan, Jessica McQueen, Kiran Sahib, and Deborah Brommer—all available from www.tapdancinglizard.com.

Henna's Secret History—The History, Mystery and Folklore of Henna by Marie Anakee Miczak (iUniverse.com): A fascinating academic study of the history and usage of the sacred henna plant; Marie Anakee Miczak is a leading authority on the subject and an accomplished henna artist.

The First British Book of Henna Art by Farah Khan (AuthorHouse): A talented British henna artist invites you to join in the beauty and magic of henna design and adornment; an excellent source of patterns and ideas.

Henna Pro Henna Designs by Sarah Ali Khan: A collection of beautiful and unique henna designs consisting of pregnancy designs, lower back and upper back designs, chest designs, designs for hands and feet, and more! What makes this book unique is that the main designs are given on separate pages for you to print out to use for tattoo transfer.

Love Mehndi by Kiran Sahib: More than eighty magnificent bridal henna patterns from a London-based expert henna artist specializing in Eastern, Arabic, and contemporary designs.

Mehndi—Art of Henna Body Painting by Carine Fabius (Random House USA): A superb book covering all aspects of henna body art.

Mehndi by Loretta Roome (Saint Martin's Press): This book traces many of the traditions surrounding the frequently used henna designs and includes some stunning photographs.

The Art of Mehndi by Sumita Batra (Carlton Books Ltd): An excellent book for design techniques or for the first steps in becoming a professional henna artist.

Magical Aromatherapy—the Power of Scent by Scott Cunningham (Llewellyn Publications): Discover how to use aromas from fresh and dried herbs and essential oils to make changes in your life. You can use them to bring you love, peace, protection, psychic awareness, happiness, joy, and more.

The Fragrant Mind—Aromatherapy for Personality, Mind, Mood & Emotion by Valerie Ann Worwood (Bantam Books): An excellent reference book that charts the various personality types, moods, emotions, and the corresponding essential oils and how they can effect change in the mind and body.

The Fragrant Heavens by Valerie Ann Worwood (Bantam Books): A perfect companion to *The Fragrant Mind*, this groundbreaking book draws on scientific and spiritual research to show the effect that essential oils can have on our spiritual progress and awareness. Worwood references seventy oils that can have a positive effect on our use of prayer, healing, and meditation.

Signs, Symbols & Omens—An Illustrated Guide to Magical and Spiritual Symbolism by Raymond Buckland (Llewellyn Publications): In *Signs, Symbols & Omens*, leading occult authority Ray Buckland describes the form and meaning of over 800 symbols from ancient and modern religions, magical traditions, and indigenous cultures around the world.

The Magician's Companion—A Practical and Encyclopedic Guide to Magical and Religious Symbolism by Bill Whitcomb (Llewellyn Publications): Includes information on correspondences.

Index

Acacia, 122, 124

Acorn, 71, 204

Aditi, 137

Aether, 136

Africa, 6, 14, 33, 41, 228

Agni Ea, 138

Air, 52, 60, 95, 103, 111, 126–127, 136–137, 146, 148, 151, 230

Alchanna, 7

Alchemical, 79, 81, 98, 105, 137–139, 157, 201, 207, 210, 227

Alchemy, 74, 78, 94, 98, 105, 107, 111, 172, 176, 225

Al-Henna, 7, 43

Allspice, 118, 122, 130

Almond, 71, 115, 122, 130

Alpha, 71

Amulets, 26, 32, 38, 60–62, 81, 86, 112, 206

Amun, 75, 109, 144

Anael, 142, 155

Anath, 15, 29, 48

Anchor, 71

Angelica, 122–124

Angels, 26, 28–29, 71, 90, 122–124, 133–135, 137–139, 141–144, 152

Anise, 115, 122, 124, 128

Ankh, 26, 71–72, 86, 201–203, 209

Ankle, 67

Ant, 71

Anubis, 86, 88, 142, 230, 232

Aphrodite, 77, 79, 95, 115, 139, 143

Apple, 73, 95, 116, 204

Aquarius, 114, 137, 144, 147, 149, 151–152

Arabic, 7, 17, 33, 43, 59, 90, 215, 235

Ares, 29, 143

Arianrhod, 137

Aries, 28, 97, 114, 138, 143, 145, 149–150

Arms, 11, 32, 42, 62, 64, 66, 83, 146, 163, 178, 195, 220, 222

Arrow, 66, 73

Asia, 6, 89

Astarte, 77, 143

Astrological, 28, 82, 89, 97, 106, 113–114, 133, 135, 137–145, 149, 219

Axe, 73

Ayurvedic, 14

Azoth, 138

Baal, 15

Baby, 38–39, 53–54, 60, 94, 213, 217–219

Back, 18, 24–25, 32, 37–38, 41, 60, 63–64, 66, 75, 81, 83, 89, 148, 159, 161, 163, 166, 169–170, 172, 213, 222, 225

Baha'i, 106

Balm of Gilead, 120–122

Bamboo, 73

Banishing, 29, 53, 86, 106, 123–125, 135, 143, 153–155, 207–208

Baraka, 59

Basil, 29, 115, 122–124, 129–130, 208, 211

Bast, 138, 141

Bat, 73

Bay, 122, 124, 126–128

Bayberry, 130

Beans, 73

Bear, 60, 73, 134, 221
Bee, 73
Bell, 74, 207
Belly, 69–70, 166, 200, 208, 215, 217, 219, 221–222
Benzoin, 114–115, 122, 126–127, 129–130, 137, 142, 200
Berber, 34, 38–39, 66
Bergamot, 122–123, 200
Bhawana, 136
Bible, 9, 47, 83, 235–236
Birds, 18, 33, 73–74, 77, 79, 86, 94–95, 138, 140
Birth, 8, 38–39, 53, 62, 81, 93, 137, 213, 217, 219
Black, 6, 14, 31, 81, 114, 122–124, 144, 149, 155, 158–159, 161, 163, 177, 179, 205, 207, 226
Black Pepper, 114, 122–124, 205, 207
Blessed Thistle, 124
Blue, 52, 54, 60–61, 81, 89, 143, 150–151, 159, 206
Breast, 69, 203, 205, 222
Brigit, 29, 138, 143
Brown, 6, 144, 147, 155, 158, 175, 187, 191, 226, 236
Buckeye, 130
Buckthorn, 122, 124
Butterfly, 72, 74
Caduceus, 72, 74, 103, 201, 203
Calligraphy, 17, 67, 87, 215, 227
Cancer, 114, 139, 141, 147, 152
Capricorn, 114, 137, 144, 146, 148–150

Cardomom, 177
Carp, 74
Cascara, 130
Cassiel, 144, 155
Cat, 74, 130, 210
Cat's Claw, 130
Cedar, 117–118, 122, 124, 126, 130, 144, 209, 231
Ceres, 136
Cernunnos, 136
Chai, 75
Chain, 75
Chalice (see also Cup), 75–76, 78
Chamomile, 114, 117–118, 122, 127, 129–130
Charms, 19, 24, 26, 34, 37, 60, 62, 64, 66, 68, 71, 73, 77, 81, 85, 89, 93, 97, 101, 105, 109, 194
Child, 33, 37–39, 45, 55, 75, 217, 219
Childbirth, 15, 37, 119, 235
China, 7–8, 74, 77, 79, 83, 98–99
Christian, 49, 101, 109
Chrysanthemum, 75
Cinnamon, 5, 113, 115, 120–124, 128, 141, 205, 211
Cinquefoil, 130
Circle, 38, 75, 78–79, 90, 97, 102–103, 108, 195, 203, 207–209, 230, 232
Circumcision, 13, 17, 39, 41
Clouds, 77
Clove, 114–115, 122–124, 130, 179, 207, 211
Clover, 77, 130, 210–211

Column, 77
Comfrey, 117–118, 122, 130
Cone, 77, 95, 169–171, 173–175, 177, 179, 183–184, 186–188, 226
Cookies, 223, 227
Corn, 77
Cosmetic, 1, 10, 13–14, 18
Crescent, 49, 78, 85, 91, 101, 204
Cross, 24, 60, 71, 76, 78, 98, 106, 108, 195, 207–209, 225, 232
Crowley, Aleister, 28, 236
Cube, 78
Cup (see also Chalice), 75, 78, 134, 161, 172, 175, 179, 181
Cypress, 7, 114–115, 117–118, 122, 144
Cyprus, 10
Damiana, 121
Decorative, 10, 50, 64, 71
Demeter, 115, 136, 144
Designs, 3, 17, 25–26, 32–34, 41–42, 45, 49, 59–60, 63–64, 66–71, 85, 97, 161, 163, 167, 171, 180, 187, 194–195, 199–200, 202–203, 206, 208–209, 211, 214–215, 217–218, 221, 223, 227, 230, 232–233
Diamond, 34, 79
Dill, 121–122, 124, 129–130
Dionysius, 136
Dioscorides, 10, 14
Disk, 60, 79, 81
Divination, 90–91, 135, 142
Diwali, 17, 27

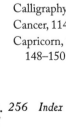

Diwali, 17, 27
djinn, 38, 45, 52–55, 57, 217, 237
Djinn, 38, 45, 52–55, 57, 217, 237
Dolphin, 79, 140
Dove, 79
Dragon, 76, 79, 124, 139, 143
Dragon's Blood, 124, 143
Dragonfly, 79
Dreams, 24, 91, 95, 110, 142, 153, 215, 233
Duck, 79
Earth, 23, 52, 67, 74–75, 77–78, 82–83, 85, 87, 95, 102–103, 110–111, 133, 136–137, 146, 148, 150, 210
Ebers Papyrus, 9–11, 235
Egg, 24, 42, 81, 226
Egypt, 7–8, 11, 13, 23, 53, 74, 83, 85–86, 89, 94, 98–99, 106, 109, 214
Egyptian Privet, 7
Eid al-Adha, 13, 15, 33, 49–50
Eid al-Fitr, 13, 15, 17, 49–50
Elements, 28, 81, 87, 95, 103, 105, 111, 134, 136, 193, 203
Essential Oils, 25, 111–113, 164–167, 169, 176–177, 179, 183, 194, 197, 221, 230
Eucalyptus, 31, 114, 122–123, 126–127, 165, 179
Eye, 15, 26, 34, 39, 45–46, 59–63, 70, 74, 79–81, 85, 97, 107, 109, 125, 187, 195, 204, 206–208, 218

Eye, Evil, 15, 34, 39, 44–46, 59–63, 70, 74, 79, 81, 85, 97, 124–125, 206–207
Eye, of Horus, 26, 63, 80–81, 207–208
Faeries, 82, 105
Feather, 82
Feet, 1, 5, 8, 11, 15, 19, 32, 37, 42–45, 62, 67–68, 152, 163, 181, 221, 232
Female, 13, 38, 44, 46–47, 52, 61, 85, 91, 94, 97, 102, 110, 134–135, 206, 219, 227
Feminine, 70, 78, 82–83, 85, 91, 95, 97, 101, 107, 134, 136, 139, 146–150, 152–153, 204, 223
Fennel, 117, 123
Fertility, 15, 34, 48, 52, 71, 73–74, 77, 79, 81–83, 85, 87, 91, 94–95, 97, 101, 142, 153, 155, 202
Feverfew, 122, 124
Fig, 82
Fig Leaf, 82
Fingernails, 9, 12–13, 17, 48, 64
Fingers, 8, 19, 58–59, 61, 63, 65, 163, 184
Fire (see also flame), 28, 52, 55, 77, 82–83, 95, 98, 103, 106–107, 111, 133, 136, 138, 145, 147, 150, 200–201, 203, 206, 221
Fish, 61, 82, 84, 140, 151, 202, 207
Flame, 82
fleur-de-lys, 82, 84

Flower, vi, 76–77, 82, 89–90, 157, 205, 218, 230–232
Fortune, 52–53, 59, 62, 67, 71, 73–74, 77, 79, 82–83, 95, 106, 131, 144, 214, 223, 231
Frankincense, 5, 114–115, 122–124, 126–128, 141, 165, 207, 209, 231
Freya, 115, 143
Frog, 83
Gabriel, 134, 139, 141, 153
Gaia, 136
Galangal, 29, 114, 122, 124
Garlic, 29, 122, 124
Gemini, 114, 137, 142, 145–148, 150–151
Geranium, 114, 116–123, 125, 165, 202
Ginger, 29, 113–114, 121–122, 129–130, 177, 202, 204–205, 211
Ginseng, 118, 121, 130, 141
God, 11, 14, 22, 29, 34, 47, 50, 52, 59, 71, 74, 78, 83, 85–87, 93–94, 97, 101, 107, 109, 115, 133, 136
Goddess, 8, 15, 48, 59, 78, 82, 85, 89, 91, 94, 99, 103, 109, 115, 142, 225
Gods, 29, 38, 53, 59, 71, 77, 99, 113, 115, 136–139, 141–144, 214, 228
Gold, 19, 24, 44, 61, 106, 139, 141, 148
Goldenseal, 118, 130
Grapes, 83

Great Work, 63, 66, 90, 98, 151, 181

Greece, 60, 86–87

Green, 5, 19, 142, 146, 151, 155, 158, 161

Gulhina attar, 6

Hadiths, 12, 235

Hair, 1, 3, 5, 8–10, 12–14, 39, 43–45, 48, 56, 64, 119, 157–159, 161, 167, 183, 220, 231

hammam, 56–57, 220

Hammer, 83

hamsa, 34, 61, 83, 227

Hand, 2, 8, 13, 34, 44–45, 61, 63, 66, 70, 83, 90, 107, 160, 175, 181, 184, 193, 203, 206, 220, 227, 230–231

Hand of Fatima (see also Hand of Miriam), 13, 34, 61, 70, 83

Hand of Miriam, 34, 61, 83

Handfasting, 97, 213, 227

Harquus, 159, 161

Hathor, 115, 143, 214

Hatshepsut, 13

Hazel, 118

Health, 6, 14–15, 46, 52–53, 55, 60, 66, 77, 81, 91, 103, 117–119, 123, 125, 144, 153–154, 157, 196, 201–202, 208, 210, 218, 220, 227, 230

Heart, 31, 34, 65, 69, 82–83, 86, 90–91, 98, 121, 144, 148, 157, 193, 195, 199–200, 203–204, 206, 208–209, 222, 230–232

Hearts, 12, 69, 91, 198, 206, 214–215, 223, 227

Hecate's Wheel, 84–85

Hen parties (bachelorette), 45, 214, 242

Henna, 1–15, 17–18, 24–25, 31–34, 37–39, 41–59, 62, 64–71, 87, 112–113, 134–135, 145, 152, 156–173, 175–181, 183–185, 187–188, 191, 193–195, 197, 199, 201, 208, 213–214, 217–223, 225–227, 229–233, 235–237

  Black, xix, 6, 14, 31, 144, 155, 158–159, 161, 163, 167, 177, 179, 207, 226

  Removing, 192

Henu, 7, 9

Heptagram (see also Septagram), 105

Herbs, 14, 25, 27–29, 31, 46, 111–113, 115, 118, 121, 124, 127, 130, 135, 165, 177, 194, 196–197, 236

Hermes, 74, 133, 142

Hestia, 138

Hexagram, 100, 105, 152, 207

Hibiscus, 121–122, 177

Hieroglyphics, 9

Hieroglyphs, 67, 85, 214

Hindu, 17, 41, 90–91, 115, 215

Hinna, 7

Honeysuckle, 122, 130, 144, 204

Hops, 118

Horn, 61, 85, 109

Horse, 51–52, 84–85, 99–100, 118, 139

Horse Chestnut, 118

Horseshoe, 85

Horus, 26, 29, 63, 75, 80–81, 109, 138, 141, 143, 207–208, 214

Hourglass, 85

Hyssop, 122, 124

Ibis, 86

India, 6–7, 14, 32–33, 37–38, 41–42, 48, 59, 83, 89, 94, 158, 169, 214, 217, 228

Indigo, 31, 158–159, 239, 245

Iris, 137

Isis, 75, 86, 109, 115, 134, 141, 144

Islam, 4, 12, 22, 33–34, 52, 54, 83, 86

Ivy, 14, 86

Jackal (see also Anubis), 86

Jacquard bottle, 169, 171, 184, 186

Jagua, 159, 161

Jasmine, 114, 117–118, 120, 122, 135, 141, 199, 201, 203, 205, 215, 221, 230

Jewish, 7, 14, 17, 34, 37, 44, 46–47, 51, 57, 61–62, 75, 87, 236

Juniper, 114, 117–118, 122–123, 125, 208

Jupiter, 65, 122, 131, 140, 143–144, 150–151, 154, 210–211, 219

Kama Sutra, 18, 32–33

Kameas (see Magic Squares)

Karwa Chauth, 17, 49

Key, 32, 71, 86, 88, 193
Khamsa (see also Hamsa), 34–36,
    59, 61, 227
Khephera, 137
Khonsu, 75, 109, 141
Knife, 12, 41, 86, 169
Knot, 86–87, 204
Kopfer, 7
Kundalini, 101
Kupr, 7
Kurdish, 37, 51
Kyphi, 11, 115, 141, 214
Kypros, 7, 10
Labyrinth, 87–88
Ladder, 87
Lady's Mantle, 118
Lavender, 114–116, 118, 120–
    122, 126–127, 165, 204, 230
Lawsonia inermis, 5, 7, 10, 158
Leaf, 82, 87, 90, 93, 158
Lebanon, 18, 51, 236
Left, 3, 38, 44–45, 57, 65, 67, 72,
    76–78, 80–81, 83–84, 88, 90,
    92, 96–97, 100, 104, 108, 163,
    165, 170, 174, 179, 186, 204,
    210, 228
Legs, 42, 49, 67, 109, 137, 163,
    220
Lemon, 31, 114, 116–118, 120–
    122, 126–127, 164–165, 167,
    169, 172–173, 176, 179–181,
    184, 188, 200–202, 205, 208,
    218
Lemon Balm (see Melissa)

Lemon Juice, 31, 164–165, 167,
    169, 172–173, 176, 179–181,
    188, 218
Lemon Verbena (see Vervain)
Lemongrass, 114, 122, 128
Leo, 89, 106, 114, 138, 141, 145,
    147–149, 151
Letters, 71, 75, 87, 195, 230
Libra, 98, 114, 137, 143, 145–149,
    151
Lightning, 87, 89
Lion, 89, 139, 147
Lizard, 89, 251
Lotus, 9, 84, 89–90, 115, 122,
    125, 135, 141, 204, 209
Love, 1, 3, 15, 33, 42, 46, 55, 60,
    69, 73, 77, 79, 83, 85–86, 90,
    93, 95, 97–98, 101, 113, 115,
    120–121, 123, 125, 130, 139,
    142, 145, 148–150, 155, 193,
    196, 203–206, 210, 213–214,
    222–223, 225, 227, 229–231
Luck, xv, 1, 24, 49, 67, 70, 73, 77,
    79, 83, 85, 91, 94–95, 99, 110,
    121, 129–131, 144, 154, 211,
    223, 227
Maat, 142
Magic, 4, 7, 19–29, 32, 34, 37,
    41–42, 50, 55–56, 59, 81–82,
    85–86, 88–91, 99, 101, 103,
    105, 113, 115, 133–136, 142,
    152–154, 157, 181, 193–194,
    196, 233, 237
Magic Squares, 88, 90
Magical Mehndi Cake, 223–225

Magician, 4, 23, 112, 134, 142,
    225
Magnolia, 119
Mah, 136
Male, 42, 52, 61, 85, 110, 206,
    219, 227
Mandala, 90, 92
Mandrake, 121–122
Manniche, Lise, 10, 237
Mari, 139
Mariamne, 139
Marigold, 122–123, 125
Marriage, 15, 33, 41–42, 44–45,
    74, 79, 86, 97, 153, 155, 206,
    214, 227
Mars, 28–29, 122, 140, 143, 145,
    149, 153, 201, 203, 206–207,
    219, 223
Masculine, 73, 77–79, 83, 85–86,
    91, 97, 101–102, 106–107,
    136–138, 145–147, 149–151,
    153, 223
Mawlid, 15
Mawlid, 15
Medicinal, 5, 9–12, 14, 193
Mehndi, 1, 7, 12, 32–33, 37,
    40–43, 47, 49, 157, 223–224,
    226–227, 236
Mercury, 28, 65, 74, 94, 122, 136–
    140, 142, 146, 148, 154, 219
Michael, angel, 139, 141
Mistletoe, 91
Money, 50, 93, 123, 125, 129–
    131, 141, 153, 211

Moon, 24, 49, 63, 78, 81, 91–92, 103, 122, 134–135, 137–141, 147, 153, 196, 199–204, 206, 208, 210, 214, 219, 225, 227
Mordants, 164–165, 172
Moroccan, 34, 53, 59, 68, 158, 165
Morocco, 34, 38–39, 42, 52, 54–55, 59, 63, 79, 171, 181, 206, 217
Morrison, Dorothy, 23, 237
Motherwort, 119
Muhammad, prophet, 5, 12–13, 56–57
Mulberry, 119
Mullein, 119
Muslim, 12, 14–15, 17, 33, 49, 57, 61, 87, 235
Mylar, 169
Myrrh, 128
Mysteries, the, 107, 153, 155
Narcissus, 131, 210
Nazar, 60, 81
Nefer, 91–92
Nepthys, 144
Neptune, 139–140, 151
Nettle, 119, 125
Newbury, P. E., 8
New-Skin, 180, 184
Night of the Henna, 11, 14, 43–46, 57, 155
Nubia, 11
Nuit, 137
Numbers, 28, 90–91, 134, 201, 203, 206–207

Nutmeg, 119, 122, 128–129, 131
Oak, 14, 71, 93, 119, 129, 131, 159
Oak Moss, 129, 131
Octagon, 93
Odin, 109, 142
Oils, 11, 25, 27–29, 31, 43, 111–113, 115–117, 120, 123, 126, 129, 135, 164–167, 169, 173, 176–177, 179, 183, 193–194, 196–197, 205, 221, 230–231, 236
Olibanum, 138
OM, 73, 88, 90, 93
Onion, 119
Orange, 6, 52, 114, 116, 120–122, 129, 131, 148, 163, 191, 200, 202, 209, 211, 218, 226, 231
Orris Root, 121–122, 205
Osiris, 11, 75, 109, 139
Ouroboros, 92, 94, 101
Owl, 94, 96, 210
Palm, 46, 63, 166, 177, 184, 203, 206, 210, 227, 230–232
Palmarosa, 114, 120, 204
Pan, 136
Paraphenylenediamine (PPD), xix, 159
Passover, 17, 24, 225
Paste, 3, 11, 15, 31, 42, 44, 46, 50, 56, 157–161, 165, 167, 169, 171–177, 179, 183–184, 187, 191, 197, 220, 226
Patchouli, 114, 120, 122, 129, 131, 202, 205, 211

Pattern, 16, 42, 45, 68, 70–71, 187–188, 217
Pear, 94
Pentagram, 100, 103, 207, 209
Peppermint, 114–115, 117, 119–122, 126–127
Persephone, 136
Petrie, William Flinders, 8
Philosopher's Stone, 81
Phoenix, 66, 82, 94–96
Pig, 95
Pine, 29, 95, 114, 117, 119, 122, 126–127, 165
Pine cone, 95
Pisces, 82, 114, 139, 144, 147–149, 151–152
Planets, 28, 65, 93, 105–106, 113, 122, 140, 193
Plants, 5, 7, 14–15, 27–29, 34, 59, 89, 95, 193, 265
Pliny, 10
PMS, 53, 134
Pomegranate, 95, 165, 176
Poppy, 95, 121–122, 204
Poseidon, 139
Power, 3–4, 15, 18, 26, 29, 59, 62, 69, 71, 73, 77, 81–83, 85, 87, 89, 91, 93–94, 101–103, 106, 109, 111–113, 124, 129–130, 141, 161, 163, 167, 177, 193–194, 201, 213, 217, 225, 233
PPD (paraphenylenediamine), xix, 158–159
Pregnancy, xix, 15, 37, 166, 197, 217–218

prima materia, 73, 81
Prometheus, 138
Protection, 26, 29, 31, 34, 37–38, 52, 57, 60, 65–67, 73–75, 77, 79, 81, 85–87, 90–91, 95, 97, 101, 103, 105, 107, 110, 113, 117, 121, 123–125, 135, 143, 153, 155, 195–196, 204, 206–207, 218, 223, 227, 231
Purim, 17, 51
Quene, 7
Quince, 95
Ra, 138, 141
Rainbow, 97
Raindrop, 97
Ram, 50, 96–97, 145, 202
Ramses, 13
Raphael, 138, 142, 154
Raspberry, 121
Red, 1, 5–6, 8, 14–15, 18–19, 28–29, 48, 52, 61, 143, 145, 153, 157–159, 163, 177, 191
Rhea, 136
Rhombus, 97
Ribbon, 97
Right, 2, 21–22, 44–45, 48, 67, 78, 80–81, 83, 90, 97, 113, 133, 162, 170, 173–174, 203, 224
Rings, 47, 65, 81
Ritual, 3–4, 8, 21, 25–28, 34, 37–39, 41–42, 46, 48, 56–57, 91, 128, 134–135, 141–144, 152–155, 157, 161, 165, 169–171, 175, 177, 179, 182–184, 187–188, 191, 205, 213–214, 217–223, 228–229, 231

River, 89, 97
Rose, 9, 98, 114–117, 119–123, 125, 136, 142, 199, 202–205, 215, 218, 220–221, 230–231
Rose Cross, 98
Rose Geranium, 114–117, 119–123, 125
Rose maroc, 204–205, 230
Rosehip, 117, 119–121, 205
Rosemary, 114–115, 117, 119–123, 125–127, 202
Rue, 125
Runes, 98
Sachiel, 144, 154
Sage, 115, 119, 122, 126
Sagittarius, 114, 138, 144, 147, 150
Salamander, 98
Salt, 55, 136–137, 180, 220, 230
Samael, 29, 143, 153
Sandalwood, 15, 113–115, 117, 119, 122–123, 125–128, 138, 142, 201, 203, 207, 209
Sanskrit, 7, 90, 93
Sassafras, 131
Saturn, 65, 122, 140, 144, 150–151, 155, 206, 208
Scales, 98, 148–149
Scarab, 98–99, 207, 210
Scorpio, 28, 99, 114, 139, 143, 145–149, 151–152
Scorpion, 11, 99, 149
Sea Horse, 99–100
Seasons, 265
Sekhmet, 89, 138, 141

Septagram (seven-pointed star, see also Heptagram), 105
Serpent, 64, 94, 99, 101, 109
Shell, 71, 101–102
Shoulder, 66
Shu, 137
Sickle, 101
Sigil, 195, 202, 204, 206, 211
Silver, 24, 61, 78, 134, 139, 141, 153
Skull, 101, 145
Sma, 100, 102, 201
Snail, 102
Snowflake, 102
Solar Plexus, 69, 206
Sole (of foot), 67
Song of Solomon, 5, 9
Spain, 7, 17, 101
Spear, 102
Spearmint, 118–119, 122, 129, 131
Sphere, 93, 102, 134
Spider, 23, 102
Spikenard, 5, 122, 129, 131
Spiral, 67, 69, 100–103, 206, 209, 230, 232
Spirit, 53, 55–56, 60, 71, 75, 79, 81–82, 86–87, 91, 103, 105, 109, 127, 136–137, 155, 193–194, 206, 219–220, 230–231

Spiritual, 11, 14, 20, 22–23, 27–29, 32, 49, 52, 66, 73, 75, 77–79, 81–83, 87, 89–90, 94–95, 97–99, 101–103, 105–107, 109–110, 113, 117, 119, 123–128, 136–138, 146, 193, 204, 208–209, 218–219, 222, 228

Square, 75, 78, 88, 90, 103, 154

St John's Wort, 125

Staff, 74, 103, 231

Star, 34, 54, 73, 78, 103, 105–106, 128, 153–155, 207, 210

Star Anise, 128

Star of Solomon, Star of David, 105

Strawberry, 115, 121, 245

Sulphur, 136, 139

Sun, 38, 63, 65–66, 69–70, 73, 75, 77, 79, 81–82, 89, 94–95, 99, 106, 115, 122, 140–141, 147, 152, 181, 200–201, 203, 206–210, 214, 218–219, 225, 227

Sword, 38, 104, 106, 209

Symbols, 3, 25–26, 28, 32, 37–38, 59–60, 62–69, 71, 73, 77–78, 81–82, 85, 87, 89, 91, 93, 97, 101, 105–106, 109, 193–196, 201, 204, 207, 210, 214, 221, 223, 227

Syria, 15, 18

Talismans, 26, 37–38, 60, 62–64, 66, 68, 71, 73, 77, 81, 85, 89–90, 93, 97, 101, 105, 109, 112

Tammuz, 136

tantric, 101, 222

Tarot, 29, 134, 137–144, 261

Tattoo, 32, 159, 251

Tau, 106, 108

Taurus, 114, 137, 143, 146, 148–151

Tea Tree, 31, 118, 165

Terpene, 163, 176

Thor, 83, 144

Thoth, 80–81, 86, 115, 134, 136–137, 141–142

Thyme, 114, 118–119, 122

Tiamat, 139

Tiger, 107, 183

Tobacco, 29, 122, 125, 143

Toes, 163

Tonka Bean, 122, 129, 131

Tree, 10, 31, 60, 66, 77, 93, 107, 111, 118, 131, 165

Triangle, 77, 81, 107, 109, 201, 206

Triple Goddess, 78, 85, 91, 109, 115

Triquetra, 108–109

Triskele (Triskelion), 108–109

Ugaritic, 15

Uraeus, 101, 108–109

Urania, 137

Uriel, 137

Vayu, 137

Venus, 65, 122, 140, 142–143, 146, 149, 155, 199, 202–204, 206, 219, 223

Victorians, 14

Vines, 42, 66–70, 215, 223

Violet, 142

Virgo, 114, 137, 142, 147–148, 150

Vulcan, 138

Walnut, 38, 125, 131, 159

Water, 11, 14, 37, 42, 46, 52–53, 57, 63–64, 79, 82, 89, 95, 98, 103, 111, 113, 133–134, 136, 139, 147, 149, 151, 173, 177, 181, 184, 191, 199, 203, 208–209, 218, 220–221, 230–231

Web, 3, 20, 23, 102, 110

White, 5, 60, 81, 134, 141–142, 149, 153, 206, 226, 231

Wicca, 109

Wisdom, 4, 22–23, 64, 66, 74, 77, 81, 86, 137, 155, 184, 236

Wishbone, 110, 210

Yellow, 5, 14, 42, 54, 141–142, 146, 152, 154

Yemen, 34

Yin/Yang, 108, 110

Ylang-Ylang, 114, 116–117, 120, 199, 204–205, 221

Zeus, 115, 137, 144

Zodiac, 98, 151, 193, 227

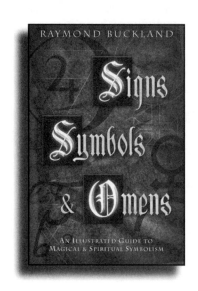

RAYMOND BUCKLAND

Signs
Symbols
& Omens

AN ILLUSTRATED GUIDE TO
MAGICAL & SPIRITUAL SYMBOLISM

Signs, Symbols & Omens

An Illustrated Guide to Magical & Spiritual Symbolism

Raymond Buckland

From the well-known zodiac of astrology to the intricacies of the Pennsylvania Dutch hex signs, the metaphysical field is replete with symbols and sigils. Many of them were incomprehensible to the uninitiated—until now. Reference more than 800 symbols in this guide by leading occult author Raymond Buckland. It includes the symbols, signs, and omens observed in virtually every significant culture and religion in the world.

978-0-7387-0234-6

$15.95 • 6 x 9 • 264 pp. • illus., bibliog.

TO ORDER, CALL 1-877-NEW-WRLD
Prices subject to change without notice
Order at Llewellyn.com 24 hours a day, 7 days a week!